"Turning human 'resources' into human 'capital'—a prerequisite to win in this era of talentism. An inspiring read for those who are trying to make a difference!"
    —**Alain Bejjani,** CEO, Majid Al Futtaim Group

"If you believe you've read all there is about the role of human capital in propelling value creation, think again. Charan, Barton, and Carey have crafted their many experiences into a compelling and concise book that frames a 'people before strategy' argument that is refreshingly new and different."
    —**Ed Breen,** CEO, DowDuPont; Lead Director, Comcast

"Engaged employees are the key to success in any business, and *Talent Wins* offers real-world insights on how to foster talent, inspire creativity, and lead winning teams for the long term."
    —**Kenneth I. Chenault,** Chairman and CEO, American Express; Director, IBM and Procter & Gamble

"Talent is the difference between a good company and great company. And nurturing talent—helping people flourish—requires continuous action, effort, and work. It is critical to the mission and the aspirations of an organization that leaders be inventing, and then reinventing, the talent development playbook. *Talent Wins* helps you do just that."
    —**Alex Gorsky,** Chairman and CEO, Johnson & Johnson; Director, IBM

"This book gives compelling arguments for treating talent management as a crucial competency for any company that wants to succeed. The authors' proposed approach is a real departure from many accepted practices in talent management. Taking their recommendations to heart will significantly change the role of CEOs as well as the requirements for HR professionals in the future."

—**Hein Knaapen,** Chief HR Officer, ING Bank NV

"Business leaders have talked about the importance of people for years but often were vague about how to turn talent into a competitive advantage. In this new book, Charan, Barton, and Carey turn conventional views about human resources on their head and create the ultimate playbook for making human capital the ultimate edge for organizations of all types."

—**William McNabb,** Chairman, The Vanguard Group

"Talented people working together is the catalyst to deliver profitable growth for the benefit of all stakeholders. *Talent Wins* provides compelling strategies and tools to continuously develop the talent in your organization!"

—**Alan Mulally,** retired President and CEO, Ford Motor
Company; former CEO, Boeing Commercial Airplanes; and
Director, Google and Carbon3D

"Millennials will soon account for over half of all workers. They want to be not only more creative, productive, and collaborative than ever before, but they also seek a greater sense of purpose and a deeper connection to their company's mission. *Talent Wins* implores senior leaders to know their employees as well as they know their finances and the capital they deploy."

—**Satya Nadella,** CEO, Microsoft

"With real-world experiences from broad industries, Charan, Barton, and Carey bring to life a game plan to identify and develop talent—and leverage that talent for winning outcomes."

—**Susan Peters,** Senior Vice President, Human Resources, General Electric

"A groundbreaking book for the next twenty years that focuses CEOs' attention on the strategic value of employees and the necessity of bringing HR into the leadership circle. A must-read!"

—**Denise L. Ramos,** CEO and President, ITT Inc.; Director, Phillips 66

"In a competitive global economy, no business can afford to leave talent on the sidelines. *Talent Wins* provides an innovative framework for cultivating talent—and shows that diverse teams are critical to unlocking an organization's full potential."

—**Sheryl Sandberg,** COO, Facebook; founder, LeanIn.Org and OptionB.Org; and Director, Walt Disney Company

"*Talent Wins* exquisitely captures the essence of creating a modern digital platform and management practices to reinvent the HR role in your company with the goal to develop, manage, and nurture the talent in today's demanding marketplace. The book includes excellent case studies and practical examples that provide guidance and insights for every executive to consider in building a successful company."

—**Ivan Seidenberg,** former Chairman and CEO, Verizon; Director, BlackRock

"*Talent Wins* can be a key to unlocking the full potential of Japanese global corporations."

—**Masahiko Uotani,** President and Group CEO, Shiseido Company

The NEW PLAYBOOK *for*

PUTTING PEOPLE FIRST

RAM CHARAN | DOMINIC BARTON | DENNIS CAREY

HARVARD BUSINESS REVIEW PRESS

Boston, Massachusetts

The web addresses referenced in this book were live and correct at the time of the book's publication but may be subject to change.

Library of Congress Cataloging-in-Publication Data

Names: Charan, Ram, author. | Barton, Dominic, author. | Carey, Dennis C., author.
Title: Talent wins : the new playbook for putting people first / by Ram Charan, Dominic Barton, and Dennis Carey.
Description: Boston, Massachusetts : Harvard Business Review Press, [2018]
Identifiers: LCCN 2017045247 | ISBN 9781633691186 (hardcover : alk. paper)
Subjects: LCSH: Manpower planning. | Ability. | Human capital. | Business planning. | Employee retention. | Personnel departments.
Classification: LCC HF5549.5.M3 C455 2018 | DDC 658.3—dc23 LC record available at https://lccn.loc.gov/2017045247

The paper used in this publication meets the requirements of the American National Standard for Permanence of Paper for Publications and Documents in Libraries and Archives Z39.48-1992.

From Ram

Dedicated to the hearts and souls of the joint family of twelve siblings and cousins living under one roof for fifty years, whose personal sacrifices made my formal education possible.

From Dominic

To all the HR leaders who've been banging the table on the importance of the talent agenda for years—thanks. You were right!

From Dennis

To my children, Matt and Maggie, who continue to amaze and inspire me, and to Donna Gregor, my assistant of over twenty years, who does all the work and gives me all the credit.

Contents

Introduction
Memo to the CEO: Your Talent Playbook   1

1.   Forge the Tools of Transformation   13

2.   Energize the Board to Help Talent Drive Strategy   37

3.   Design and Redesign the
     Work of the Organization   57

4.   Make HR a Source of Competitive Advantage   79

5.   Unleash Individual Talent   103

6.   Create an M&A Strategy for Talent   131

7.   Drive the Talent Agenda   155

Notes   169
Index   171
Acknowledgments   177
About the Authors   179

Introduction

Memo to the CEO: Your Talent Playbook

What is the key to the future of your company?

Better yet, *who* is the key to the future of your company, and what are you doing to unleash his or her potential?

Most executives today recognize the competitive advantage of talent, yet the talent practices their organizations use are vestiges of another era. They were designed for predictable environments, traditional ways of getting work done, and organizations where lines and boxes defined how people were managed. As work and organizations become more fluid— and business strategy comes to mean sensing and seizing new opportunities in a constantly changing environment, rather than planning for several years into a predictable future—companies must deploy talent in new ways. In fact, talent must lead strategy.

That's a radical departure from the past. Something this big is a job for the CEO. Simply put, reimagining and leading a people-first company cannot be delegated to anyone else in the organization. In the past, some "people initiatives" were viewed as "soft" or "feel-good" efforts that didn't merit the CEO's full attention. That won't suffice. What's needed now is something altogether different, and far more demanding. In our opinion, putting talent first means a complete transformation of the way most companies have done business for decades.

That's why the time has come for you—and every CEO who intends to succeed in his or her job—to take charge of talent. You must deploy talent as successfully as you deploy capital. You must know your employees as well as you understand your finances. You must shape an organization that empowers those employees to create as much value as possible.

This is complicated stuff. But companies that manage the transition from strategy-first to people-first will reap enormous rewards.

That's why the three of us have come together to write this book now. We have spent decades helping top business leaders execute their strategies. Ram has been a confidant to the CEOs of some of the world's biggest corporations and their boards, advising them on how to create value and helping them execute their most significant strategic shifts. Dominic, as the Global Managing Partner of McKinsey, has hundreds of CEOs who turn to his firm when it comes time to change strategy or transform their business model. Dennis, the Vice Chairman of Korn Ferry, a premier recruiting firm, works closely with boards and CEOs to ensure that their companies have the right directors, chief executives, and top leaders in place.

We have *never* come across a moment like this, when virtually every CEO we work with is asking a daunting set of questions: Are my company's talent practices still relevant? How can we recruit, utilize, and develop people to deliver greater value to customers—and do so better than the competition? How can I be sure that I have the right approach to talent—and the right HR—to drive the changes we need to make?

These questions recognize a basic truth of our time: Talent has never been more important to the success of a corporation. Talent is king. Talent, even more than strategy, is what creates value. The implications of this are profound, and are what this book is about.

You Must Manage Human Capital as Wisely as Financial Capital

Consider the board game Risk. Players have a simple goal: take over all the countries of the world by using their army to wipe out the armies of the other players. When several players compete, there almost always comes a point when the weakest have been destroyed and two or three players are left to face off. None of the survivors of the early skirmishes is an overwhelming leader; with armies strewn across the continents, each competitor has a chance to win.

Luck, in the form of good or bad rolls of the dice, will have a part in determining the winner. But the outcome will most depend on who best deploys his or her armies. When so few competitors are left, each player may get a fistful of troops each turn. Do you gather them into a single country abutting your opponent's weak spot? Do you spread them widely to distribute the risk? Do you emphasize your strongest sectors? You will win or lose depending on how you deploy your troops.

The analogy to business is clear: deployment of assets is the way you win or lose. But which assets? Most businesses have focused for years on the deployment of capital, with good reason. McKinsey consultant Stephen Hall, along with his former colleagues Dan Lovallo and Reinier Musters, studied more than 1,600 US companies, looking at how their financial results lined up with their movement of capital. They found that companies that reallocated financial capital aggressively from one division to another, based on market opportunity and performance, were worth 40 percent more after fifteen years than companies that had been relatively passive. The top third of their sample returned 30 percent more to shareholders than the bottom third.

The best CEOs constantly review and reallocate financial capital, withdrawing funds from some places and adding more somewhere else. Security analysts watch this closely, rewarding companies that aggressively move capital, like Alphabet, Google's parent. But Google is just as bold when deploying its other critical resource: people.

Now, let's be clear: Deploying human capital is very different from deploying financial capital. Dollars and euros will go where you send them—and they won't complain, of course. People, on the other hand, want to have a say in their fate. And at a time when talent is in such high demand, you must allow—and even encourage—people to have their say if you hope to attract the very best in your field. So, the successful deployment of talent is now largely a matter of creating an environment where the interests, ambitions, and innovations of people constantly shape the strategy and future of the company. Companies manage this challenge in myriad ways. In Google's case, for example, talent deployment emerges from a workplace where people have considerable leeway in deciding what projects they want to work on. In other companies, like Haier and McKinsey, a talent market determines deployment.

Our goal with *Talent Wins* is to provide a playbook that will help you deploy human capital as effectively as you deploy financial capital. The structure and practices that make sense for your company are not necessarily the ones that will work for another company. This is not a one-size-fits-all kind of book, because there's no one-size-fits-all, universal solution for maximizing the potential of something as complicated as talent. Yet as the three of us interviewed hundreds of top leaders for this book (CEOs, CHROs, CFOs, directors, and others), we discovered a set of principles shared by the most forward-thinking companies, principles that provide the foundation of such talent-driven organizations as ADP, Amgen, Aon, Apple, BlackRock, Blackstone, Google, Haier, Johnson & Johnson, Marsh, PepsiCo, Telenor, and many others you will encounter in this book. *Talent Wins* will show you how these principles can drive exponential growth at your own company.

Talent Wins: A Playbook for Transforming and Leading a People-First Company

Talent Wins will show you what it really takes to create and lead an organization that lives by one simple but profound conceit: people, not companies, generate value. Acknowledging the

FIGURE I-1

The new playbook for putting people first

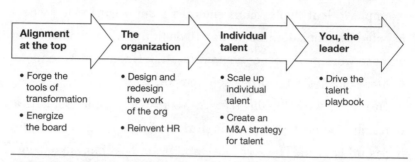

Alignment at the top	The organization	Individual talent	You, the leader
• Forge the tools of transformation • Energize the board	• Design and redesign the work of the org • Reinvent HR	• Scale up individual talent • Create an M&A strategy for talent	• Drive the talent playbook

importance of talent is easy. Transforming a company into a talent-first organization is hard. Our talent playbook will guide you through the complex process. We have broken it down into seven steps, as shown in figure I-1, each of which features creative, actionable ideas for leaders who are ready to transform and steer a people-first company.

In the first chapter, our three steps spotlight tools that every CEO needs to effect a talent-first transformation. This is not a mission you can attempt unarmed and solo. First, you must forge a "G3"—a group of three people consisting of you, your CFO, and a CHRO who is as committed, talented, and empowered as the CFO herself. This is the core executive group of your new company, a powerful tool that will lead the transformation and ensure that talent is allocated wisely and in sync with capital. Second, you need to develop both a roster of the top talent in your company (hint: it's not your organization's top tier) and a deep understanding of the people on it. It may sound strange to think of a roster as a tool, but the people on it will be those whose deployment has a disproportionate return on investment. We call them the "critical 2 percent." If you don't know them and understand them well, you can't deploy them as effectively as possible. The third tool you need at your disposal is what we call "talent technology," software applications that elevate your ability to identify, recruit, and support talent both inside and outside your company. Without a strong, effective, and supportive core at the top, a thorough sense of your most valuable talent, and the digital tools that any modern company must have, your transformation will fail. This is a more radical transformation than anything you've tried before—don't launch it without the tools for success.

In the second chapter, we take you through four steps to ensure that your board of directors is aligned with and is supportive of your effort to have talent drive strategy. Handled properly, the board can be another important tool in your transformation. Your directors need to be steered from the traditional definition of TSR (total shareholder return) to a new one: talent, strategy, risk. This new TSR is the appropriate metric for any company that believes value is created by talent. But taking it to heart entails a profound, company-wide shift in mindset, attention, energy, and the content of work. We take you through the details of how to bring directors along and make them comfortable with and supportive of this shift. One example: today's compensation committee, which is often focused narrowly on pay for you and a handful of others, should be renamed and refocused into a talent committee, knowledgeable enough about those in the critical 2 percent to advise you on their deployment.

The first two chapters are about aligning the top of your company—your CHRO and CFO team, your board, your top talent. The next two are about the organization of the corporation— how you should be thinking about structure and about HR if you are to manage human capital like you manage financial capital.

Chapter 3 shows how to create a more horizontal, flexible structure that connects and multiplies talent. In most corporations, everything—work, decision making, compensation, career paths, even who gets the best computer—follows a vertical path. But hierarchy can isolate and bury talent. Instead, a people-first company relies on the work of small, cross-functional teams that come together, disband, and reform as suits the nature of their work. Flattening the organization will stimulate creativity and personal growth. It creates speed. Think of this as a process of unbundling the existing structure to take advantage of the power of collaboration and unleash a remarkable new corporate energy. This isn't a one-time fix. In fact, you'll have to organize and reorganize your talent in sync with today's high velocity of change. To remain on offense, your organization should always be optimized to the moment. There's no single model of how to do this, but in chapter 3 we introduce the three factors that support any talent-first organization: agility, platforms, and meaning.

In chapter 4 we tackle a second organizational imperative: the radical reinvention of HR. The time has come to remake and releverage HR into much more of a creator of value and competitive advantage. We know that dozens of books have pushed for a reinvention of HR. This book is different, because we place that reinvention in the context of a broader, urgent transformation of the entire organization. The reinvention starts, as we note in chapter 1, with the CHRO, who must be a full and equal member of the G3, armed with business acumen that's every bit as valuable as the CFO's. Going forward, it will be critical for CHROs to have line or budgeting experience on top of more-traditional expertise in things like judging people's talent accurately and placing them in the right jobs.

But this reinvention extends well past the CHRO. You and the CHRO must make tough decisions about what administrative tasks in HR can be automated, outsourced, or offshored. Here, too, new software is transformative: Johnson & Johnson, for example, has automated two-thirds of the processes HR once handled. Don't think of this as an evisceration of HR; in fact, many leaders should spend more time with HR, and more CEOs should have HR experience. Think of this instead as a strategy for unleashing talent on the things that allow a company to compete: identifying the critical 2 percent; keeping the talent pipeline filled; reading the global talent market; shaping the internal org structure and adapting it in flexible ways to the changing demands of your business; creating flexible, rational performance criteria and ensuring that pay is used wisely as a motivational tool for the employees who matter most; and helping define, and support, the strategic direction of the company. This is work that will help the entire company perform better.

In chapter 5, we move from the organization to the individual. This chapter offers a road map for continuously scaling up people's talent in rewarding and productive ways. Skill obsolescence is a nerve-racking reality, so talent development is more important than ever. To succeed and grow in an economy that has decimated predictability, your company must make three critical moves to unleash its talent: Your most vital people must be in roles where they can create significant value. They must be freed from bureaucratic structures designed for a different era. And they must be afforded the training and opportunities to continually expand their skills. New software can help, but none of this is possible without your full attention and commitment.

No matter how well you develop your internal talent, the ever-shifting nature of business today means that you'll regularly have to look outside the company for talent that lets you jump on new opportunities. The war for extraordinary talent is intense now, and all the data suggests that it will only become tougher. In chapter 6, we look at what it takes to create an M&A strategy for talent, so that you can find, attract, and successfully integrate talented people from the outside. To make this work, you first need to develop your peripheral vision, that ability to see trends developing along a wide spectrum and to figure out which ones apply to your business. In a world where industry borders are increasingly porous, peripheral vision is a must-have skill. Second, you need to embrace new ways of acquiring talent, like the acquihires that are so popular in Silicon Valley. Finally, you must put your CHRO at the center of your new M&A activity. Your CHRO should have the clearest vision possible of the world of outside talent. He or she should also lead the integration of the new talent you bring in. Well over half of all corporate acquisitions fail, usually because the needs of top talent at the acquired company have not been fully considered. Putting the CHRO at the center of all talent M&A will go a long way toward addressing that problem.

The final chapter is about you. Implementing this new talent playbook will change everything about how you lead. You will become the architect of the recruiting process, the monitor of its output, and the chief recruiting officer for critical talent. You'll develop a GPS for external talent. You'll make the board your talent-management consultant. You'll get granular on issues you may once have left for HR, so that you are sure you're maximizing the impact of the critical 2 percent and the growth and continuous learning of the 98 percent. You will have to find ways to lead by example, since your clearly signaled, enthusiastic commitment is critical to establishing the right tone across the entire corporation. Putting the CEO talent playbook to work will draw on much of your time, energy, and focus. You'll have to figure out what current responsibilities you're going to hand off so that you can give talent the time, energy, and focus it demands. Chapter 7 provides an outline of the changes we think you will need to make, along with an "operational checklist" of the ways your own job will be altered as you steer the company.

Elevate Human Resources to the Same Level as Finance

Our playbook will help you transform your company from a strategy-first business to one that puts people first. In doing this, you will be elevating HR to the same level as finance, a shift that is long overdue but essential now that you must manage human capital with the same rigor you apply to financial capital.

The three of us have been thinking about this monumental shift for some time now. In a way, the genesis of this book occurred in 2014, when Ram wrote an essay for *Harvard Business Review* called "It's Time to Split HR," which simply said it's time to reinvent the HR function.[1] A year later, the three of us followed up on Ram's piece with an HBR article called "People Before Strategy," which outlined a more proactive and strategy-driven role for the head of HR.[2] With this book we expand the lens even further. We are making the case that HR, armed with first-rate business acumen and a keen sense of how the finances and talent of the company can work in sync to rapidly accelerate value creation, must be elevated to the level of finance. This is an absolutely necessary shift for any CEO trying to lead a broad transformation of the company into a talent-driven operation, and it is why we say that CEOs need to lead the change.

We are not the first, of course, to write about the challenges associated with managing people and human resources. Our work stands on the shoulders of such giants in the field as USC's John Boudreau, Wharton's Peter Cappelli, Harvard's Paul McKinnon, and the University of Michigan's Dave Ulrich, who have written excellent books and articles on best practices in the evolving world of human resources.

This book is different. By outlining the CEO playbook, we focus broadly on how you must reimagine your company to successfully manage, organize, hire, track, monitor, and support the people who ultimately are the value creators in this new digital age. The hundreds of executives we have interviewed for this book are at the leading edge of linking talent to value creation. Their stories and our experiences are the source material for this book.

You know that talent is the secret to competitive advantage in the twenty-first century. Yet most companies—including yours, perhaps—operate by talent practices that are stuck in the twentieth century. *Talent Wins* is the essential guide for you and every other leader who wants to change that, who understands that the time has come to build a new type of company— one that puts talent at the very center of value creation.

Forge the Tools of Transformation

In April 2015, Peter Zaffino, then the CEO of Marsh, the giant insurance broker and risk manager, did something simple but radical: he invited his CHRO Mary Anne Elliott and then-CFO Courtney Leimkuhler to sit together with him to review the business. What was radical about this? Well, Zaffino had been meeting regularly with Elliott to review talent. And he'd been meeting every quarter with Leimkuhler for numbers-driven operational reviews. But he'd never brought the two of them together for a company-wide review. By bringing people and numbers together for the first time, Zaffino was convening what we call a G3—and nothing was ever the same for the top team.

"The whole meeting took about fifteen minutes," says Zaffino. Their work was high-level stuff, built on a simple design. They drew a two-by-two chart on a white board. On one side of the vertical axis, they listed issues relating to business performance; on the other, organizational concerns. Above the horizontal axis, they noted things that were going well; below, things that weren't. The simplicity of the chart, combined with the power of having both finance and HR in the same room, made some major trends at Marsh pop: the business was effectively controlling costs, and its products were differentiated, but the company was still adjusting to the fact that fees were being unbundled across the industry. Unit leaders were committed to the company's goals, but some weren't pursuing growth opportunities as aggressively as they could.

Together, the three executives adjusted a new sales incentive plan that Elliott was about to introduce, so that it would better align with Marsh's overall business goals and would encourage the team to deliver near-term results *and* focus on the future. They also prioritized a problem that they'd previously put on the back burner. They all knew that regional business leaders weren't being transitioned quickly enough, but only when the executives looked at the problem together could they acknowledge that this issue was a real drag on the business. They agreed to attack the problem immediately.

"When you understand which things on the organizational side are really advancing business performance," says former CFO Leimkuhler, "it makes it easier to prioritize." In that small group, core issues were tackled head-on. "It would be unwieldy to have this discussion with the full executive committee," adds Leimkuhler.

After that first meeting, Zaffino decided that the G3 would become a permanent fixture, the core management group of the company. The trio met formally each quarter, and interacted constantly outside that formal setting. Conversing frequently, Leimkuhler and Elliott gained a fuller understanding of the business and became their own team of two. "We already ran the business with disciplined processes," says Zaffino, who left Marsh for AIG in the summer of 2017. "But this G3 process provided us with a terrific lens into the business without adding bureaucracy."

The G3 that Zaffino created is the most important and most powerful tool at the disposal of any modern CEO. As CEO, you have two critical resources: money and people. Getting the people who manage those resources in the same room with you is the only effective way for you to link the company's financials with the people who produce them. In this chapter, we'll delve deeply into the G3: we'll look at its mandate, what makes a G3 effective, and what it means to elevate your CHRO to the same level of importance, responsibility, and trust as your CFO. We'll also look at the second and third critical tools you must forge before attempting to transform your company into a talent-first powerhouse: a roster and deep knowledge of the key employees who can have an outsize impact on the company's success—the group we call the critical 2 percent—and the talent technology that will transform your understanding, awareness, and management of talent. With these tools in hand, you can start building a people-first company.

Create Your Most Important Tool: The G3

Let's take a moment to consider just how ambitious a G3 can be. The G3 is most effective when its mandate is vast: the group should lead the way on anything where the deployment of talent influences the company's results. In other words, the G3 will tackle almost anything you would tackle as CEO.

During formal meetings and informal get-togethers like those that characterized the interaction of Zaffino's trio, the G3 will work to ensure that talent and finance will be appropriately linked in all mission-critical decisions, operations, and future planning. This trio of top executives must dissect past events to understand the root causes of a business's failure or success. It must prescribe actions to improve performance, and make certain that the organization has the talent it needs to move the business forward. It must know the talent well enough to predict the likely outcomes these individuals will produce. By tightly linking finance and talent, it ensures that the organizational side is considered through a holistic lens, and that financial projections are informed by the reality and potential of talent. The multidisciplinary combination of CEO, CFO, and CHRO can help guarantee that your company stays on offense.

By putting talent and finance on equal footing, the G3 will change the way and sequence in which these critical matters are discussed. A G3 leadership team doesn't turn to personnel and organizational issues only *after* having reviewed financial results and strategic initiatives across each business unit, as typically happens today. Talent is not some discrete item on your agenda. Talent is inextricably tied to every item on the agenda.

Think of the G3 as the central brain trust of a talent-first organization. (You might want to keep the general counsel or chief risk officer close on big decisions if that suits your business, but it's the ongoing CEO-CFO-CHRO linkage that's crucial.) Effectively deployed, the G3 is the mechanism that will create the future of your organization. It can be the multiplier of your capacity, time, and capability, as illustrated in the following example.

Vinod Kumar, the CEO of India's Tata Communications (Tatacom), didn't set out to create a permanent G3, but he adopted one after working on a specific project with his CHRO and CFO in 2012. At the time, the prices Tatacom could charge corporations for the communication, computing, and collaborating infrastructure it sold were dropping precipitously. Kumar knew that the only way to offset the price cuts was to offer new, higher-value-added services, but these would be based on capabilities the company didn't yet have. Tatacom would have to hire new, more experienced talent from the outside—an expensive proposition—and do so in a hurry.

Since the dilemma was one that seemed to pit finance against HR, Kumar called in CHRO Aadesh Goyal and then-CFO Sanjay Baweja. A series of intense, three-person meetings led to a strategy that made sense from both the finance and the HR side. Tatacom would eliminate redundant roles while moving some of the displaced workers to areas with high demand. This cut staffing costs by 7 percent, and Tatacom poured the savings into salaries for new employees with the different sales, marketing, and technology skills it needed.

Pleased with that short-term success, Kumar then tasked the G3 with a set of long-term goals, including cutting costs and remaking the company culture to ensure continuous improvement. Kumar, Goyal, and Baweja expanded their reach by setting up a cross-functional team that employees could join part-time. Ultimately, five hundred people temporarily signed on, and the team cut well over $100 million from costs, often with programs that the G3 could never have imagined on its own. What started as an experimental gathering of three executives had become a company-wide cultural transformation.

The success of the Tatacom G3 is a clear example of what can happen when a company's CHRO is elevated to the most senior level. Working so closely with the CEO and the CFO, CHRO Goyal improved his business-analysis skills and his ability to better link talent and business. In fact, Kumar's faith in his CHRO grew so strong that he recently put Goyal in charge of a company subsidiary that offers payment solutions to banks, a growth target for the business. Needless to say, the CFO-CHRO-CEO dialogue is now an institution at Tata Communications.

Elevate the CHRO

The G3 must be a triumvirate of strength, three top leaders who can be supportive of one another while being honest and frank. Ed Breen, who turned around Tyco before signing on as CEO of DuPont, says, "You're going to be more brutally honest. The CHRO and the CFO might have to tell the CEO that someone he's very close to in the organization isn't an A-plus player. That's how you'll come to better decisions." At Veritiv, Chairman and CEO Mary Laschinger relies on a G4. "The general counsel, the CFO, and the HR leader provide me with objectivity across the organization," she explains. "The HR role is just as important as those other roles."

For this to work, you must make clear that your CHRO is every bit as critical as your CFO. Ever since the rise of the "Super CFO" back in the 1980s, the CFO has been in "the room where it happens," as they sing in the musical *Hamilton*.

Bringing the CHRO into a G3 is an equally momentous shift. It's an acknowledgment of the fact that talent consideration must be a critical part of every important decision.

For years, consultants and pundits have talked about elevating HR to the highest level of the corporation. If you truly believe that talent drives your company's value, you'll understand why the time has finally come to make that happen. Do you have the right people in your company's key roles? Are your best people all gravitating toward a certain trend, and should the company steer that way? Who are your future leaders? What companies are wooing your best employees, and what does that tell you about your industry's direction? Who is holding back the creation of more business value, and why? Why are some of your businesses positive or negative outliers, and how much of that performance is attributable to the executives you have put in place? Critical business questions are almost always critical talent questions. That's why including the CHRO in the company's cockpit is no longer an option—it's an imperative. "People allocation is as powerful as financial allocation," explains Aon CEO Greg Case, who works closely with CHRO Tony Goland and CFO Christa Davies to make sure the multinational has the right talent to meet the challenges of the future. "We work together to make talent decisions and integrate solutions. Pure capital allocation is essential, but that's not enough. Do we have the right talent in place? How should we think about talent development? If you've got an opportunity to acquire a company, do you have the right people in place to do the deal and operate it afterward? It's not a matter of getting input from my team so I can make a decision. The three of us work together as peers and answer those strategic questions as a team."

Of course, for the CHRO to play such a critical role, he or she will have to be well versed in all aspects of your business. This explains why more companies are filling the CHRO position with someone who has had line responsibilities, rather than simply promoting the highest person on the HR career ladder. A modern, empowered CHRO must have a deep understanding of business, as well as expertise in linking it to people. Forget the idea of a CHRO who bothers herself only with administrative tasks such as payroll, workplace regulations, and benefits. You need a CHRO who outsources or delegates those traditional HR tasks, and spends most of her time developing strategy and talent as part of the G3. This shift is already on: CHROs we've interviewed say that they now spend some 70 percent of their time on strategy, building the organization for the future, and talent (searching for it, recruiting it, and comparing it against that of the competition). Alan Mulally, the straight-talking former CEO of Ford, has a succinct way of describing the potential of a great CHRO. "CHROs need to be dynamite businesspeople," says Mulally. "The best ones become unbelievable business strategists."

Foster the G2 within the G3

As we said above, and as we reiterate throughout the book, deploying finance and talent together creates exponential power. This is true within the G3 as well. Brought together, your CHRO and CFO can be thought of as the two legs that allow you, the CEO, to walk. They will play off one another, learn from each other, and make up for each other's weaknesses. Paired as full partners in a G3, they can accomplish far more than either could alone—by ensuring that the company's financials and the company's people are continually, inextricably linked. They are a powerful G2 inside the G3.

The recent turnaround at McGraw-Hill is an eye-opening example of the power of a successful CFO-CHRO team. At the beginning of this decade, CEO Terry McGraw's company was in a bind: its S&P Rating Services was under fire from regulators for its ratings of mortgage-backed securities that helped create the financial crisis. Its educational-publishing division was languishing. And the company's stock had plummeted from $70 to $17 per share. Wall Street viewed McGraw-Hill as a conglomerate with assets that weren't synergistic. Terry McGraw saw the need for something new—to take action and be bold.

In 2010, McGraw sought help from two outside hires: John Berisford, his CHRO, and Jack Callahan, his CFO. Although both spent most of their careers at Pepsico, they didn't really know each other. That didn't stop them from quickly forging a tight relationship and becoming a de facto G2. They understood what their CEO wanted: their outsiders' perspective on a new path forward for McGraw-Hill and a complete review of how to unlock value. "It was a treasure hunt for facts," says Berisford.

Looking across the organization, the duo found one problem after another. They benchmarked industry costs, only to discover that McGraw-Hill was the high-cost player. The company was top-heavy, with a bloated corporate structure and a workforce that needed retooling. Most employees had been at the company for life. "The paternalist nature of the company served it very well for a long time," says Berisford, "but you wouldn't call it the strongest meritocracy on the planet." The company's back-end IT-support operations had ballooned to 1,400 people.

Middle management had metastasized, with some people having as few as one or two reports. Everywhere they looked, Berisford and Callahan found unnecessary cost and complexity.

The two men often met for coffee in Callahan's office, where they'd flag several issues that were top of mind. Two or three times a month they'd go out for dinner. They were in and out of McGraw's office as well. The frequency made it easy to express their thoughts, such as questioning whether the company's three main businesses—education, financial ratings, and media—should stay together or be split off. After five months, their initial inkling became a conviction: the company should be split. Based on their findings, the board decided to divide McGraw-Hill into two stand-alone businesses: the regulated financial business, and everything else. "Even in board meetings," Berisford says, "Jack and I worked together leading discussions of whether we had the right structure and how to get more growth out of the business."

Now Berisford and Callahan tackled the dual challenge of breaking up the conglomerate and cutting costs. Taking into account salaries, benefits, and incentives, they knew that half of the company's $2 billion in total costs could be attributed to people. Yet they had little visibility into the details. "If we wanted to know the cost of the finance department," recalls Berisford, "and everyone has a different title, well who knows?" Adds Callahan: "Imagine trying to allocate a billion dollars of people cost against a revenue stream, without really knowing the profitability of anything." To have a clearer lens into the business, the duo implemented HR tools such as Workday and PeopleFluent. They made the HR and finance teams start using the same numbers. "The comp group in finance and the one in HR used to use their own math," says Callahan. "Now the teams work together and use one set of numbers that are vetted by both teams." Consistency and visibility allowed the duo to answer a variety of personnel questions: Does compensation match performance? How might specific personnel changes affect the bottom line? Remedies were divvied up—Callahan got the facts, and Berisford figured out the human equation. When the facts showed that one of the lowest-margin businesses had too many layers of management and an incentive cost structure that was unaffordable, the two leaders attacked the problem to find a solution.

Along with all the cuts, Berisford and Callahan had to do some organization building as well. Moving from a portfolio company to a centrally operating one required building up certain support functions and outsourcing others. Readying the education business to be spun off meant creating a leadership team that could stand on its own.

Did all their efforts pay off? In 2010 when Berisford and Callahan arrived, the revenue of the company was $6.2 billion. After all the restructuring, the new, slimmer McGraw-Hill had annual sales of $3.2 billion. Five years later, revenues had rebounded to $5.1 billion, and the company's market value had quadrupled. Today the company's market value is approaching $40 billion, from the $9 billion it had been when Berisford and Callahan joined.

The McGraw-Hill case is a textbook example of how the G3 should work. The G3's mandate was just as broad as the CEO's—turn around a sluggish enterprise. The CEO elevated the CHRO, set a tone of openness and intellectual honesty, and fostered a close rapport in informal chats and formal meetings.

The CFO and CHRO developed their own alliance. They welcomed incursions onto their "turf," and served their CEO by refusing to be "yes men." In fact, they often pushed back repeatedly with the conviction of facts and the strength of their partnership on matters that were emotionally charged, like the sale of the education unit and J.D. Power. They were able to do this because they understood the leverage of controlling the most important forms of capital—financial and human. The partnership remained strong after McGraw retired in 2013, with Doug Peterson becoming the new CEO. Berisford was emboldened to advocate for a strategic move that most CHROs wouldn't touch, precisely because of his close partnership with CFO Callahan. "Because of my relationship with Jack," he says, "I could keep asking questions about strategic moves like J.D. Power without being thrown out of the room." "If finance and HR aren't talking," adds Callahan, "then they aren't creating new value."

Identify and Cultivate the Critical 2 Percent

The G3 may be your company's central brain trust, but without the support of the critical 2 percent—those employees who create disproportionate value—it is powerless. The potential of your company depends on this group. (That 2 percent figure is merely a guideline; in big corporations, the "2 percent" may be a group of fewer than two hundred people.) So, the very first task of the G3 is to identify those people who in the right roles will most accelerate your company's growth. Once you know who they are, you can maximize the value they create by understanding their skills and needs, listening to what they're telling you, continuously developing their skills, customizing their career plans, and constantly assessing their roles in the future of the company.

Let's pause for a moment to acknowledge that you must also develop the skills of the other 98 percent of your people. But in this book, we'll talk far more about the top 2 percent than about the other 98 percent. There are three reasons for this. First, plenty of other books do a good job of suggesting ways to motivate, train, and incentivize your staff at large. Second, this book is focused on how you can transform your company into a talent-first organization, and aligning this top cohort with your effort will exponentially increase your chances of success. Ed Breen at Tyco, Lou Gerstner at IBM, and Steve Jobs at Apple are all examples of CEOs who turned around their companies by leaning heavily on their key talent. Third, and most important, the three of us believe that your company's strategy, direction, and success should and will be determined by the work and vision of these people. Deploying them smartly is critical; to do so, you must know their strengths and weaknesses well.

So, who makes up the 2 percent in your company? That's not such a simple question, because the 2 percent is most definitely *not* a group of employees with the fanciest titles in your company. Instead, this high-leverage group can include key designers, scientists, salespeople, up-and-coming leaders, influencers, integrators, and support staff tucked away in unglamorous corners of your company. Apple's Jonathan Ive is an obvious example of a 2 percenter, as is star cardiologist Steven Nissan at the Cleveland Clinic. But how about the navigation-software experts at UPS? Though software engineers make up a tiny percentage of the UPS workforce, their in-house routing software—which directs drivers to take as few left turns as possible to minimize time spent at red lights—saved millions of dollars in fuel costs per year, and multimillions of employee hours. The head surgeon at a hospital might be a member of the 2 percent, but so might the worker three layers down who negotiates with the government and insurance providers for discounts, a job that has a huge impact on the facility's profits.

Value creators aren't necessarily inventors of new products, great strategists, or those most adept at ascending corporate ladders. Whatever their position, they are people who get to the heart of issues, reframe ideas, create informal bonds that encourage collaboration, and make the organization healthier and more productive.

According to one McKinsey study, about 70 percent of senior execs are wrong about who is most influential in their organization. Some of your 2 percenters are likely to be key actors within the company's social networks who know how to spread information judiciously and get things done. Often, these are veterans whom newcomers turn to for advice on how to advance projects through the organizational cross-sections. Other 2 percenters might include a savvy analyst who provides valuable insights into a diverse set of data, a programming expert who is remarkably fast, even that charismatic person who creates an infectiously encouraging workplace around him. These people can be powerful change agents, and using them to communicate with the organization is often faster than going through the official org chart. According to the McKinsey study, one pharma CEO who decided to spread a message about change via the company's informal influencers needed only 2.3 steps to reach an employee, versus the 4.5 it would have taken through traditional channels. This means your message moves faster, without the degradation of an extended game of "telephone."

Clearly, identifying the true value creators requires hard work and a deft touch. It also requires a sense of *where* to look. The G3 must pinpoint the company's crucial decision nodes, the places in the organization where important choices are made by people who can drive tremendous value. Who is really exercising power at those key points? (Often, it's not the official decision maker.) How do decisions at those nodes create or destroy value? Knowing where to look can lead to extraordinary gains.

A few years ago, Sandy Ogg, in his role as operating partner at Blackstone, was working with the leadership of one of the private equity giant's portfolio companies. The company's value agenda was to increase earnings from $600 million in EBITDA to $1 billion, while shifting the multiple from 8x to 10x. Using an approach that he had developed while working with other companies in the portfolio, Ogg identified the pivotal roles in the 12,000-person organization that could drive this $400-million opportunity while preserving the $600 million. He boiled it down to thirty-seven critical positions, one of which could single-handedly generate $60 million in EBITDA. That translates into $600 million in value when the business is sold for the 10x multiple. The men and women in those thirty-seven critical roles held the fate of that investment in their hands. Ogg, along with the company CEO and the rest of the Blackstone team, took the time to ensure that those thirty-seven positions were filled with leaders who were up to the task ahead. Their investment in lining up the right talent in these critical roles paid off handsomely.

That's a good example of the power of truly knowing your 2 percent. But this is a tool that needs to be honed constantly.

Identifying your 2 percent is a job that never stops. At Johnson & Johnson, CHRO Peter Fasolo watches his top performers like a hawk to make sure that, as he puts it, "The company is building capability for the future and getting ready for the new digital and health-care economies." As Fasolo analyzes his top 2 percent (whom he defines as the top fifty players in his company), he constantly asks himself: Are these fifty really the shapers of the future? Are they movers and shakers?

He also constantly asks himself, Do we have the skills we need in-house, or should we hire from outside? Identifying your 2 percent may well expose gaping holes in your arsenal that can be filled only by bringing in talent from the outside. So this ongoing internal audit must be accompanied by an expansive external one. The best companies regularly scan fields far from their own to be aware of talented executives in entirely different industries whose novel approaches might reinvigorate a company. It may well be that a key member of your 2 percent doesn't even work for you now.

Digitize HR

The third tool you must have in your kit is one that didn't even exist a few years ago. Until recently, talent- and HR-oriented applications lagged other enterprise software. In the past few years, however, developers have started delivering a slew of programs that help you learn much more about a greater number of your employees. Any G3 that wants to seriously lead a company where talent leads strategy must arm itself with this cutting-edge, talent-oriented, data-based IT, which lets you understand your workforce better than ever before.

The software revolution is late getting to HR, but attention is finally being paid. In 2015, venture capitalists invested $2.4 billion in 383 HR-software deals in the United States, up 62 percent from 2014 and eightfold since 2011. That's a reflection of pent-up demand. In one recent survey, just 8 percent of HR departments said they had the software they needed to do a good job analyzing the performance of their employees. In another, 75 percent of HR departments reported that getting such applications was a top priority.

Given that level of need and investment, HR software will improve considerably over the next few years. But what it can already do is quite impressive. Just as the advent of spreadsheet applications (e.g., Lotus 1-2-3) and enterprise financial systems helped fuel the rise of "Super CFOs" in the 1980s, today's new digital tools will help CHROs make themselves indispensable. Digitally literate companies are already using HR analytics to improve their talent spotting, recruiting, hiring, onboarding, training, retention, performance reviews, and pay. We are entering an era in which data-driven software analysis will become a standard part of any talent decision.

A few quick examples will give you a sense of what this new software can do:

> *Recruiting:* Startups such as Gild, Greenhouse, Entelo, and Jobvite link social media, résumés, and other public data to find job candidates. Other companies are using artificial intelligence to sift through people's social media (with their permission) to identify jobs that match up well with their skills and personalities. Data analytics can also reduce unconscious biases that creep in when recruiting is handled intuitively.

Retention: By crunching massive amounts of data, new HR software can help you discover who might be considering leaving your company and why. It can signal when it's time to give a restless member of the 2 percent a bigger job so that the person doesn't seek one elsewhere. The analysis can also help you discover small adjustments that may have an outsize impact on employee satisfaction. Google, which may be more advanced in its use of talent-oriented software than any other company, discovered that new mothers had inordinately high attrition rates. By lengthening their paid maternity leave from three months to five, Google cut that turnover in half.

Career development: New software applications look at a variety of data over time to discover talented internal candidates whose growth should be accelerated. The revealing data can be drawn from résumés you've got stored in HR, employees' LinkedIn profiles, or even their email habits. For example, VoloMetrix, a startup Microsoft acquired in 2015, looks at one-on-one interactions with managers, time spent in meetings, email exchanges, and performance reviews. This kind of employee monitoring can help identify potential leaders in a company.

Performance management: Mobile apps can reduce dependence on the annual performance review by encouraging continual constructive feedback. At GE, managers meet regularly with direct reports to update priorities based on customer needs. As GE's Leonardo Baldassarre and Brian Finken explained in a 2015 *Harvard Business Review* article, "Development is forward looking and ongoing; managers coach rather than critique; suggestions can come from anyone in an employee's network . . . At its core, the approach depends on continuous dialogue and shared accountability."[1] A simple smartphone app tracks the process for each employee, organizing voice and text inputs, documents, and even handwritten notes. GE claims that the teams that have adopted the approach have driven a fivefold productivity increase in the past twelve months. GE is now rolling out the program to the entire company.

Culture transformation: Driving a people-first organization means learning, and then fostering, the kinds of behaviors that help your employees do their best collaborative work. Data analysis can help. For example, Harry's, a Manhattan startup offering shaving supplies to subscribers, adjusted the layout at its headquarters based on data from heat-mapping cameras that revealed things like where the most productive teams would meet and what areas of the office were going unused. A large European retail bank commissioned a Boston startup, Humanyze, to help it understand why some branches were performing brilliantly while others were doing poorly. Humanyze went into several branches that paid workers a commission on the number of small-business loans they issued and asked employees to wear high-tech Bluetooth badges equipped with a mic and an accelerometer. The startup discovered that at the chattiest branches, employees had banded together and opted for a shared bonus plan. The shared incentive structure fostered communication, and the communication led to greater productivity. The most talkative branches had the highest per-capita revenue. Data in hand, the bank instituted the shared incentive structure at its other branches. Says Humanyze CEO Ben Waber: "When we tested this concept, branch sales went up 11 percent. Across the bank, this amounted to hundreds of millions of dollars of new revenue." A study at Google revealed that the company's most productive teams were ones in which everyone had an opportunity to speak, in which most employees had a high EQ, and in which dialogue was conducted in a way that made all members feel safe. The company then applied those findings to new groups forming around the organization.

That's just a sample of what's possible with this new technology. Some companies are laying the foundation by building what we call a digital people platform. Once you create it, and establish the protocols for collecting data, you can amass and quickly analyze data from the farthest reaches of your organization. With this data foundation in place, you can leverage other tools and processes. It's a big, costly undertaking, but trying to get ever greater results out of patchwork legacy systems is unlikely to get you to the same place. The biggest problem: cleaning up old databases that have different formats and inconsistent information is a time sink. One CHRO spent nine months trying to clean up his company's data before halting the effort. He eventually decided his team's time would be better spent ensuring that all new data is accurate and consistent. One key to doing that: link payroll and HR data. Since employees like to get paid, they tend to make sure that every line of payroll data is accurate.

Jan Siegmund, the CFO and corporate VP of ADP, concurs with the idea that finance and HR should have the same data to foster good decisions. Siegmund was chief strategy officer before moving into the finance role, and is deeply involved in talent development. "Before I became CFO, there would be a discussion of, 'How many people do we have in this business unit?'" says Siegmund. "And it was challenging, because our financial forecast would not match our people forecast." Now HR and finance use the same planning system.

PepsiCo's senior vice president of global HR operations and shared services, Shakti Jauhar, encountered the data-harmonization issue when executive vice president and CHRO Cynthia Trudell asked him to enable HR transformation through digital systems to increase efficiency and meet twenty-first century demands. Jauhar assembled a team of HR and IT experts. Their goal was to migrate all the in-house HR systems to the cloud, build a core platform that included HR information about each employee, and create a single privacy-protected site online where everyone in the organization could have access to data that he or she needed from HR. It wouldn't be an easy task. PepsiCo had multiple HR systems around the globe. Global data reporting was difficult, and even sometimes not available. With over 260,000 employees, says Jauhar, "It was clear we couldn't harmonize historical data and had to start from scratch and collect the data on the new platform."

The journey began with data entry self-service in the United States—where employees, managers, and HR entered the relevant information through a user-friendly portal designed to ensure that jobs, titles, pay categories, and work experience were consistent. "The organization was very supportive of this first step in transformation," says Jauhar, "because having trustworthy data makes completing day-to-day tasks more efficient." PepsiCo has been updating its HR platforms since 2010 and has now deployed a global platform that captures the data of all its employees.

Getting the core platform in place and the data accurate took years. Now PepsiCo is focused on enhancing the technology by adding mobile apps, analytic scorecards, and even robotic process automation and artificial intelligence to the platform. Leaders at all levels can use data to manage talent in many ways, such as succession planning, internal recruiting, managing and tracking headcount as well as turnover, and generally work more efficiently. "The goal," says Jauhar, "is to have data and analytics available instantly and easily."

Turning HR into a data-driven entity required commitment by PepsiCo, but Jauhar estimates that PepsiCo will get a significant ROI. "The HR department of the future," says Jauhar, "will be more efficient and act like a true business partner supporting the growth of our business."

A digital transformation as thorough as PepsiCo's; the identification of your critical 2 percent; the formation of a G3: these are the foundation of any talent-first organization. You need each of these three building blocks in place before you can start to allocate people as well as you allocate capital. Once they're in place, the ripple effect on the rest of the corporation will be profound. As we'll see in the next chapter, those changes will begin inside the corporate boardroom.

Getting Started

Transforming your company into a people-first organization is an arduous, time-consuming job. It isn't something you should jump into unprepared. In fact, we believe you need to have three tools at your disposal to get started.

The first and most important tool is the G3 consisting of you, your CFO, and your CHRO. For this to work, the CFO and CHRO must be star performers who can learn each other's language and dive into each other's business. They are your key players in allocating talent in sync with capital. Ultimately, the success or failure of the G3 is up to you. You must encourage—insist and act on, in fact—honest, open feedback, and you must ensure that the G3 meets regularly, with an agenda of meaningful, actionable items focused on the deployment of human capital. You should also encourage your CFO and CHRO to strengthen their own relationship, and empower them to lead the way on major issues. That's what it takes to sculpt a G3 that is as cohesive and efficient as the ones at Marsh and McGraw-Hill.

You'll need to forge two other tools as well. The first is a thorough identification and understanding of the superior value creators in the company. This is the roster of the talent in your company that can create exponential value. We call these people the critical 2 percent. The challenging part of forging this tool is finding the *real* talent in your company—not just the employees who have risen up the corporate ladder. The G3 must survey far reaches of the company to find these people, and look with an open mind. You're quite likely to find unlikely people creating unlikely value in unlikely places. Please note: this is a job for all three members of the G3. It's not something that can be left to the CHRO. You are looking for value creators, and your CFO is the one with the data that differentiates between someone who looks good on paper and someone who truly produces.

The third tool is easy to describe and hard to install: the technology to support your talent-driven transformation. Working with a CIO who truly understands the business, you'll need to procure and propagate software applications that inform and improve a broad set of talent-oriented processes. Five or ten years ago, HR software was a mess. But in the past few years it has improved so much that it is now a necessity.

Armed with these three tools, you'll be ready to transform your company into a talent-driven enterprise. As we'll see in the next chapter, all three tools will play a critical role in aligning the board of directors with your reinvention of the organization.

2

Energize the Board to Help Talent Drive Strategy

This chapter will look at how you can align your board of directors to support the needs of a people-first company led by talent. You can't meaningfully empower the talent below without the full commitment of leadership above. This is a top-down revolution. As CEO, you must ensure that your board of directors is entirely committed to your talent-first transformation, and fully supports its success. Just as the G3 must align management with the idea that linking talent and finance reigns supreme, you as CEO must enlist the board in your effort.

The role of the board is often underplayed in discussions around talent. Boards, of course, have a litany of issues to squeeze onto their time-constrained agendas: operating reviews, cyber-security, financial reporting, shareholder activism, regulation, and compensation. Keeping commonplace administrative tasks at bay is a constant challenge. Talent discussions are largely limited to CEO succession. But as the CEO of a talent-first organization, you can't let your board remain a strategy-first body. That misalignment at the top of the organization will weaken your efforts to elevate talent, because the information the board requests, the questions it asks, and the comments it makes to the CEO and the top management team have an outsize influence on what happens inside the company.

Your job is to help the board see that talent is *the* value creator, and therefore belongs at the top of the board's agenda. Getting it there may take time and commitment, because you're asking for a change in mindset, not just a practical shift. Boards are proud to have expanded their contribution from ensuring compliance to providing advice on strategy and risk, with the goal of driving the greatest total shareholder return (TSR). You, instead, are trying to get board members to focus on talent as much as strategy, and to assess the risks associated with both. Talent, strategy, risk: you want the members of the board to make this new TSR at least as important as the other one they already worry about. You want the board to become a powerful tool to help you realize and sustain a talent-first organization.

A committed board can help you recruit, maintain, and motivate your critical 2 percent. Directors can help ensure that the company never has weak performers in critical roles. Their support sends a message to both employees and the investment community that your transformation is serious and promising. Their commitment will help you squash standard operating procedure.

The great majority of directors are unaccustomed to playing such an active role in talent management. According to a recent

McKinsey survey of corporate directors, most believe they are effective on strategy, while only 5 percent feel they are doing a good job developing people and ensuring that the company has a strong, healthy culture for those people. They do understand that a sea change is taking place—for the first time in the survey's history, directors say they want talent to become as much of a priority as strategy. They know that individual talent can create inordinate value, and they recognize the cost of ignoring it. Conor Kehoe, who for many years led McKinsey's practice on boards, says, "Up until now boards considered talent to be a management problem and didn't focus on it. Now directors are becoming more concerned about culture. They're worried about the kind of behavior that led to the global financial crisis and want to make sure they protect the company's and the board's reputation."

As CEO, you'll have to guide your directors to the best way for them to help you with talent. Using examples from a few companies that have successfully created talent-first organizations, including GE, Google, and others, we've developed a clear game plan you can follow. It encompasses what we call "the four R's": reintroduce, reorganize, reprioritize, and retell. Let's start with the first, the reintroduction of your CHRO to the board of directors.

Reintroduce

Sure, your directors already know your CHRO. But what do they think of him? In an interview a few months before his death in 2016, the late Randy Macdonald, who had been CHRO of both IBM and GTE and had served on the boards of Delphi and Time, told us, "When someone enters the boardroom as an HR person, he's probably held to a higher standard, because of cynicism and skepticism of the role of HR. There's somewhat of a bias as to what value an HR professional can really bring to the table. So I think the first thing that CHROs have to prove is that they're not there to just wave the HR flag." In many companies, HR has not been made a full partner on the key decisions regarding a company's fate, and HR's presence in the boardroom has been limited.

But if you are committed to having talent drive strategy at your company, you'll need to ensure that the board sees your CHRO as a key partner who drives the creation of value across the enterprise. You'll need to clearly explain to directors why you created a G3, and why the CHRO is as critical to the enterprise as your CFO. "The CEO really decides which members of management are in the boardroom for which discussion," says Laurie Siegel, the ex-CHRO of Tyco who is now a director at CenturyLink, FactSet, and Volt Information Sciences. "Very often, the CEO will turn to the CFO or general counsel to ask a question—and stop there. As a director, I often ask for the CHRO to be there as well. When the reaction is, 'I don't know if this HR person deserves a seat at a board meeting,' well, it's time to find a new CHRO." Gaining the full respect of the board of directors is another reason you need to be sure that your CHRO is a top-notch, seasoned executive.

A first-rate CHRO is most effective when he or she works with a board of directors that sees talent as its primary responsibility. Their mutual focus on talent ensures that discussions of strategy are never far removed from discussions of people. Bringing the CHRO into the boardroom deepens your collective analysis. "The conversation with a CHRO," says Siegel, "is not, 'We can't do it.' Instead it's, 'Here's how we can get there.' What you want is a CHRO who is a problem solver, not a deal killer." That's another reason why we believe the best CHROs are likely to have line experience running a part, or parts, of your business. The better they understand the ins and outs of your business, the better they can help you find and nurture those individuals who will create outsize value.

At more and more top companies, CEOs who have created a strong dialogue between the CHRO and the board are getting results. At Blackstone, for example, the CHRO plays an active role in assessing the performance of the CEOs of Blackstone's portfolio companies. He understands strategy well enough to know when certain CEOs don't have the skills a company needs, and his relationship with the board is so strong that the directors trust his analysis. At Norwegian mobile-telecom giant Telenor, the CHRO works hand-in-hand with the board. So when the company promised to double the number of women in management positions— the kind of pledge that is often unfulfilled—the CHRO made sure the company delivered. Taking the time to develop a good relationship between your CHRO and your board makes both parties stronger allies in your effort to drive transformation.

Reorganize

The second step we advocate has both symbolic and practical value. You need to reorganize the board of directors so that it becomes an engine for your talent transformation.

As a first step, we urge you to rename the compensation committee, and give it a new mandate. Just as many audit committees have evolved into bodies focused on strategic financial allocation, the compensation committee must evolve into a group focused on the deployment of talent. That's why it should be given a new name, such as the talent and rewards committee, or perhaps the people committee. Our research shows that many forward-thinking companies are already doing this.

The name change has symbolic value. Existing compensation committees are noteworthy now as the vehicle by which a CEO gets paid. If they ever make the news, it's often for paying their CEO some exorbitant sum with little regard to performance. A talent and rewards committee, on the other hand, promises to focus on a wider group of executives, whose compensation will depend on performance.

Far more important than anything symbolic, of course, is the tangible change that will follow the name change. A look at the GE board's management development and compensation committee (MDCC) is the best way to get a sense of just how ambitious and transformative this change can be. The MDCC starts every meeting with a leadership discussion—not a compensation discussion, as is common with many other boards. Through development, the directors come to know the strengths and weaknesses of the company's senior-most leaders. CHRO Susan Peters and her HR team present the board with all kinds of information about these key players, both individually and in aggregate. Is this cohort—GE's version of the 2 percent—being properly incentivized and rewarded? If top employees leave the company, why did they go? Is their departure an indication of a greater trend? Who best fosters creative talent and leads their team with accountability? Armed with detailed knowledge, the MDCC works with Peters to zero in on questions such as these, with special emphasis on the top twenty-five officers. Peters lets the board know about any significant changes in the group; promotions, lateral moves, big incentive raises, and, of course, firings are all discussed with the board. The board will even approve the addition of any new officer, whether brought in from the outside or promoted from within. "We get their perspective," explains Peters. "They say, 'Have you thought of this,' or they tell us what they think we got right or wrong about a personnel move. They help us think strategically about how someone will fit with a business and with the company's other leaders, and whether we're moving someone too soon, or not soon enough."

This kind of interaction and detailed talent discussion is more than most companies get from their boards. But GE pushes each director to become engaged at an even deeper level with talent. Each is required to make two visits a year to some of GE's far-flung facilities, such as an oil and gas business in Houston, an aviation factory in Ohio, or a healthcare unit in Sweden. These visits are typically conducted by a small team from the board. Directors have dinner the evening before with the business CEO and spend the next day on business topics with the leadership team. These hands-on visits make tangible the directors' sense of GE's talent pipeline. Later, if Peters proposes a promotion or new assignment for a key executive, it's more than likely that the board will have had some personal interactions with the candidate.

The payoff of such deep involvement is not as tangible as, say, a discussion in which the board recommends a major strategic shift. But it may be more important. In an interview with the *McKinsey Quarterly*, David Beatty, a Canadian executive who has served on more than thirty-five boards over a fifty-year career, describes GE's board as exemplary: "GE . . . is a talent machine. The board's contribution to the future lies less in the arena of business strategy and more in talent development and managerial succession. Directors see GE as an incredible university of capable people whose talents they develop. The oversight of that function, with respect to the future of the company, is intense and highly value added, versus the ability to say we should get out of credit, we should be doubling turbines, or we've got to move more deeply into China."[1]

A board that's focused on talent is a board that's focused on the future of your company. That brings us to another important consideration: Are your directors the right people for a talent-led transformation? As CEO, you want a board that understands and is committed to your vision for the company. As we've discussed, the shift from a strategy-led company to a talent-first company requires a profound change in mindset. Most directors will welcome the change. But some may be stuck in the past, while others may not have the experience you need. A good board should challenge you—that's constructive. But an ongoing debate with a few dissidents about the very nature of your transformation is a distraction you can ill afford.

Reprioritize

Creating a talent and rewards committee and integrating your CHRO into critical board discussions sends a clear signal to the board that talent is king going forward. Given that, what exactly do you want from your refocused directors? What are their new priorities?

We think there are three items that must be covered at every meeting of your board of directors: CEO succession, the health of the critical 2 percent, and diversity. Making these agenda items mandatory is the only way to ensure that the board has a broad understanding of the strengths and weaknesses of your team. It creates a foundation of knowledge about the company's talent, so that deliberations on any matter will always be accompanied by an educated discussion of personnel. Put simply, any discussion about any strategic option must be accompanied by a discussion of whether the company has the financial *and* human capital it needs.

CEO Succession

Here's an incredible piece of data: according to a 2014 survey by the National Association of Corporate Directors, two-thirds of companies have no formal CEO-succession plan. This seems an almost criminal abdication of fiduciary responsibility. A 2015 Korn Ferry study is almost as depressing: it found that only one out of three leaders at companies with such a plan are satisfied with it.

As we said earlier, creating a thriving talent-first organization is a top-down revolution. If you and your board don't have a good idea of who's going to succeed you, you clearly aren't committed to prospering over the long haul. Your succession should be one of your first orders of business. Apple's Steve Jobs didn't truly understand the need for this until he first got cancer, in

2004. When he came back to work the following summer, he insisted that Apple's directors confront the succession question head-on, and so they did: CEO succession was a central agenda item at every board meeting until his death. Insiders knew for years that Tim Cook would eventually succeed Jobs, smoothing the transition at a company so identified with its founder that many pundits predicted its demise. Apple's subsequently becoming the world's most valuable corporation is proof of the benefit of that seamless succession.

The CHRO should keep the board informed about inside contenders. It's her responsibility to make sure the board has a constantly updated list of candidates—well before the CEO announces his or her intention to step down. The CHRO and the CEO should collaborate with the board on the creation and continual updating of a list of criteria for the "perfect CEO," focusing on the skills and attributes the company will need in the future—not now. The CHRO needs to make sure that directors get plenty of exposure to candidates with such skills and attributes, so they can make a sound judgment when the time comes.

Yet another reason you need a powerful, confident CHRO with serious, valuable experience is to help the board design a succession process that avoids the most common pitfalls. It's typical, for example, for directors to fall in love with a candidate early, based on superficial information and impressions. A rigorous process will keep the board focused on specific demonstrations of leadership qualities that show whether someone has the character, judgment, demeanor, and intuition needed for the job. The CHRO should also be prepared to offer her own point of view on the candidates. "These are billion- or multibillion-dollar decisions, and it's worth slowing down and looking at the evidence," says former CHRO Sandy Ogg, whose responsibilities included oversight of the eighty or so CEOs running Blackstone's portfolio companies. "Someone comes back from an interview and says, 'He's a good guy. Let's hire him.' It's a billion-dollar decision, and we're going to base it on 'good guy'?"

Dan Phelan, the ex-CHRO of GlaxoSmithKline, led the drug maker's board through succession planning in the mid-to-late-2000s. Knowing that CEO Jean-Pierre Garnier intended to step down at some point, Phelan took the directors on a deep dive at multiple board meetings. Those conversations led to a set of criteria that Phelan calls "two plus two plus two": the ideal candidate would have experience running two business segments, working in more than one country, and serving at least two functions. Sir Andrew Witty, who took over from Garnier as CEO of GlaxoSmithKline in 2008, filled the bill. He had worked in both sales and marketing; served in the United States, Singapore, and South Africa; and led teams focused on respiratory and HIV/infectious diseases.

"As CHRO, you have to get the board to look rigorously at potential CEO talent," says Phelan. "You have to get them focused on placing even stronger people in the important jobs."

The Health of the Critical 2 Percent

Phelan's point is a sound reminder: any discussion of CEO succession is a discussion of the critical 2 percent. Who are your strongest internal candidates? Are they being given the challenges they need to prove their leadership qualities? These are questions that can be answered only through rigorous, consistent evaluation of the critical 2 percent. If you're a talent-first company, you can hardly leave these discussions to those moments when a CEO transition seems imminent.

It takes a strong CHRO to lead meaningful board discussions of your company's top talent. Directors won't necessarily push for all the information that's needed to make educated talent decisions. "Some boards don't ask enough of their CHRO," says Nancy Reardon, a former CPO of Campbell's and Warnaco, who's currently on the boards of the retailers Big Lots and Kids II. "Sometimes they focus too narrowly on comp and the design of the comp program." It's up to the CHRO, says Reardon, to get the board to think "bigger and broader."

"Not all boards are as nuanced as they should be," adds Bill Schaninger, who leads McKinsey's HR practice. "For example, most look at succession as a structure issue rather than focusing on, say, the twenty-five jobs that will create the most value." You and your CHRO should push the board toward the same holistic view that you apply.

Doing this will likely entail giving your directors far more detail about people than you have in the past. For example, a discussion about complaints the company is receiving on its customer hotline might seem too small-bore for the board of directors. Not so, says Reardon: "Conversations like that can lead to broader issues about retention and employee engagement. The board should know whether the company is perceived as a go-to company by prospective hires, or a place to be avoided." As directors made clear in that most recent McKinsey survey, they feel ill-equipped to guide the company on personnel issues. Well, it's up to you and your CHRO to give them the information they need. What kind of culture are you trying to build? Do you have the same kind of depth in manufacturing as you do in marketing? Are you weaker than your competitors in a critical technology job category? A board that's conversant with these kinds of questions is taking talent seriously. Consider this: You wouldn't hesitate to give your directors considerable detail about a critical manufacturing failure. Why hesitate to give them great depth about critical talent, which can have an even more lasting effect on your company's fortunes?

At the very least, your CHRO should take the board through a thorough review of the critical 2 percent—or some manageable but significant tranche of that group—every six months. Are their skills what you need to ensure future success? The rationale for such rigor is indisputable: "Get the top team right and your company will be okay," says McKinsey's Schaninger. "But if you get it wrong, the company will never overcome it. A CEO and the board can't be better than their team. It's like being an editor and having a bunch of bad writers." Don't stop at CEO succession: assure the board that you have "if hit by a bus" plans for the top 25 or 100 employees in the company, and that you're tracking potential external candidates as well as insiders.

Hein Knaapen, CHRO of the Dutch multinational ING Group, leads talent discussions with the board every two months. His stringent talent-management system focuses on whether the company's leaders have the capability to create other leaders, and whether those emerging leaders have the digital skills they'll need to move the company into the future. It's a system that led him to discover a particularly difficult personnel dilemma that he took to the board in early 2016.

What Knaapen revealed to the board was that ING was losing a lot of its younger talent. These digitally savvy junior managers, whose enthusiasm and expertise inspired other potential leaders, were leaving the company at five times the rate of senior executives. There simply weren't frequent enough vacancies in the senior ranks to let the company's up-and-comers come up, so they left for better jobs—with advancement—elsewhere.

That was bad enough, and at first glance the solution Knaapen proposed seemed almost worse. Given the onset of fintech, the inevitable digital transformation of most insurance and finance functions, and the eventual replacement of human employees with machines running on artificial intelligence, the company's future depended on a substantial influx of these very young, tech-savvy managers who were instead fleeing the company. What was needed, Knaapen believed, was a housecleaning of senior managers to make room for more junior talent. Essentially, Knaapen was proposing the replacement of many loyal employees possessing vast institutional knowledge with youngsters whose skills the company needed for the future.

This is exactly the kind of deep problem that is best handled by a knowledgeable board matched up with an expert CHRO. This kind of profound change demands rigorous board discussion, and Knaapen got it. With top management and the board in sync, ING launched its transformation. In the United States the attrition rate for senior managers is already going up, and young, rising stars are getting promoted. In Europe the process is slower, because "there is more entitlement for people who have held their jobs a long time," says Knaapen. In both regions, Knaapen has asked his board to use its extensive network of contacts to help situate the displaced senior managers at other companies.

Directors who are deeply informed about your company's talent will help you through such wrenching decisions. They can also help you recruit the talent you need. "Our board members can operate like a highly effective search firm," says Don Gogel, the CEO of private equity firm Clayton, Dubilier & Rice. "There's nothing like recruiting an executive who worked for you for a long time, particularly in some functional areas where you know that he or she is both capable and a great fit."

Diversity

Gogel's remark raises an interesting question: Can directors who love to recruit "an executive who worked for [them] for a long time" help you drive diversity through the ranks? After all, at this point it's obvious that a diverse workforce is critical to the future success of almost all companies. What role should a board full of directors who may not have risen in particularly diverse workplaces play in your effort to increase the standing of women and minorities at the company?

Once again, you'll need an honest dialogue between a strong CHRO and an informed board. While something like 50 percent of ING's employees are women, the percentage declines significantly as you go higher on the org chart. CHRO Knaapen has made it his personal responsibility to raise that number. In many cases, he says, he's fighting unconscious biases. While the board and senior management have agreed to hire women who are competing with men whose experience or talent is only marginally better, getting that to happen when it's time to offer a job is a challenge. Knaapen has developed a keen nose for such moments. Since directors respect his business skills, they pay attention when he speaks up. And Knaapen knows how to contextualize such decisions in no-nonsense terms. When a woman recently emerged as a top candidate for a job in the critical 2 percent, Knaapen put the decision in a way that made the stakes clear for the CEO and the board. "She might seem junior," he said, "but if you look at the facts of her background you will see that she's qualified for the job." He then added: "Plus, if you don't create an opportunity for her, someone else will."

It helps, a lot, if your board is as diverse as your ideal workforce. Telenor, the Norwegian telecom giant, which has 214 million mobile customers in thirteen global markets, has embarked on an ambitious effort to transform its workforce for the digital future. One example: just 5 percent of Telenor's senior leaders currently have technology backgrounds. By 2020, the company hopes to have that number up to 50 percent. It also hopes to increase the proportion of female leaders from 22 percent to 30 percent over that same time.

That's a daunting task. But Jon Erik Haug, Telenor's EVP of group people development, is working with a board that's ideally suited to the task. Four of the board's nine directors are women. The chair is Gunn Waersted, a preeminent Norwegian banker who also leads what the company now calls the people and governance committee. (Yes, it used to be the compensation committee.) Perhaps as a result, the company has woven diversity efforts into its proposed transformation. Executives from corporate headquarters, in Fornebu, Norway, are regularly sent to positions abroad, while executives from abroad are constantly flown in to Norway to educate headquarters on the best way to market to the foreign executives' respective countries. Generous maternity policies that are par for the course in Norway (including a six-month leave with pay) are helping distinguish Telenor abroad. "What we see," says Haug, "is that by focusing on gender we can stand out in some markets, like Asia, because our competitors are not focusing on it. In Pakistan, Telenor has become one of the most popular places to work because of the way they treat women." While it's still in its early stages, Haug's initiative is truly transforming Telenor into a workplace of the future, which will be both more diverse and more tech savvy.

Telenor is operating on the belief that its future depends on having the right kind of diverse workforce. It's a perfect example of why you want a strong and diverse board focused on your critical talent priorities. On the Telenor board, talking constantly about the composition of the workforce—and especially of the critical 2 percent—is an entirely natural way of addressing the future of the company. Without board support for Haug's ambitious efforts, Telenor might have become yet another of the many, many companies that have failed to increase the diversity of their leadership. It's not a coincidence that the boards of most such companies are inordinately populated by white men.

Retell

The top of the company also must align behind something else: the story you're going to tell investors. If you're leading a talent-driven organization but talking strategy-first to Wall Street, there's a disconnect between your company's public and private personae. That's not good for investors, your company, or your workforce.

Telling investors about talent seems like a risky tactical change. Why would a company in, say, the semiconductor industry want to position itself in a way that seems more suited to a movie studio announcing its latest slate of star-driven features?

There are several answers to this question. For starters, shifting to a story built around talent is a sign of the times. Some companies already include slides about their key talent in their quarterly presentations. Financial analysts know the impact people like Jony Ive, Astro Teller, Sheryl Sandberg, and Andy Rubin can have on a company's valuation. The phenomenon is hardly limited to tech: the performance or career peregrinations of Wall Street stars, fashion leaders, and even manufacturing pros can affect share prices as well.

But your company's talent narrative isn't just a story of stars. In fact, in times of great turbulence it can be a sign of stability. GE has made its deep talent-development efforts part of its narrative for years. GE stock has had its challenges, of course. But the company's education efforts at its Crotonville, New York, facility and its history of always having great talent at the ready give investors confidence in GE's management pipeline. Google's track record of giving great leeway to its talented employees is equally well known. At one point, employees were even encouraged to spend 20 percent of their time working on their own pet projects. Investors have applauded CEO Larry Page's effort to rein in some of the company's more outlandish experiments, but they wouldn't want to see the company reduce its commitment to innovation. Analysts have come to expect the unexpected from companies like Google, Amazon, and

Apple, and are apt to forgive the occasional failure, because the companies' talent-first models have produced one unexpected innovation after another. At these companies, there's a well-established narrative history of the power of talent.

Getting Started

To get the board of directors behind your effort to transform and lead a talent-driven company, it helps to remember that you're about to ask them to do something new. Most boards don't focus on talent as intently as you want yours to. So even if the directors are eager to take on more responsibility, they may not know precisely how to help you.

In this chapter, we've looked at four steps that will help you get the most out of your directors. First, reintroduce them to your CHRO. They already know your CHRO, of course. But do they know him or her only as the "people person" or, rather, as a critical strategic partner of yours? In many cases, we suspect, it's the former. Make sure they understand that you are managing this transition via a G3 in which the CHRO is a full and equal partner with you and the CFO. Give your CHRO ample time presenting to the board, to demonstrate his or her thorough understanding of the business. This will elevate the dialogue about your talent initiative and help dispel the misconception that the CHRO is "just" a people person.

Second, push to have the compensation committee renamed and refocused as the talent and rewards committee. This is a powerful way to symbolically align directors with your effort. It will also have tangible ramifications as you tackle your third task, reprioritizing the directors' responsibilities. You should insist that reviews of the critical 2 percent, CEO succession, and diversity become more important items on the board's agenda. As these items assume centrality, you will benefit more and more from board members' wide web of connections outside the company and outside your industry.

Fourth, encourage the board to support your effort to build a new, talent-first narrative around your company. Investors will always want to hear about great results. But a narrative that shows off companies as magnets for the very best talent is becoming increasingly compelling. It's a story that assures investors that your company will be a value-creation dynamo no matter how your business changes.

Once you feel that the top of the company is aligned with your planned transformation, you can move on to the next stage of the new talent playbook: reshaping your organization into a talent-first workplace.

Design and Redesign the Work of the Organization

Imagine a company at which the CEO devotes half his time to an eclectic group of thirty-eight employees who aren't his direct reports, who inhabit all sorts of nooks and crannies in the organization, many far from the executive suite. Picture a leading multinational where employees decide for themselves which team they'd like to join, and which projects they'd like to attack. How about a company divided into some two hundred customer-facing units, each with its own pay scale and work methods, each so talent-driven that employees are given the right to fire their unit leader?

These aren't far-out fantasies: such companies exist today. Organizations that want talent to drive strategy will look radically differently from the hierarchical corporations of the past, the kind laden with multiple layers of managers—as many as nineteen in one case we found!

When strategy was paramount, organizations were designed for control, with little attention paid to the velocity of decision making or the agility needed to adjust on the fly to external changes. Strategies were portfolio- or product-driven, not based on the goal of treating each customer as a unique individual (what has come to be called N=1). Clearly, that's a paradigm for an era that has disappeared.

No single organizational model has arisen to replace the old hierarchy. But alternative ways of designing work are emerging and succeeding. In this chapter, we'll look briefly at the nature of this change, and then we'll go inside several companies that have attempted reorganizations that put talent first. All are works in progress, because in a world of unpredictability, reorganization is a way of life. While there's no set model for this modern corporate organism, there are three attributes that all leading-edge companies build in: they are organized for agility, for platforms and networks, and for meaning. Any twenty-first-century company that puts talent first needs a structure that incorporates all three.

Be as Agile as Facebook

Agility is often seen, incorrectly, as the opposite of stability. In fact, as you'll see in this chapter, true agility will make your company more—not less—stable than a traditionally hierarchical organization. As McKinsey's Wouter Aghina, Aaron De Smet, and Kirsten Weerda have written, agile companies have "a fixed backbone" of structure, processes, and governance to support "looser, more dynamic elements that can be adapted quickly to new challenges and opportunities." Structurally, more people are deployed in customer-facing teams while fewer people attend to centralized oversight of corporate profit, strategy, and direction. Major decisions become the responsibility of select, efficient, cross-functional committees, while the great majority of the rest are delegated to empowered teams and individuals. Where they can, these companies create signature processes that differentiate them from the competition, but they don't try to prescribe the details of how their many teams get work done. The result is a company where employees know "this is how we do things around here," and yet feel empowered to come up with creative solutions to the rapidly evolving challenges they face.

Facebook is a great example of a company built for agility. We think of it now as one of the four most important American companies in consumer technology (along with Alphabet, Amazon, and Apple), but just a few years ago a slew of naysayers declared that the party was over for CEO Mark Zuckerberg's social network. In 2011 and 2012, pundits believed that Facebook was hopelessly behind in the race to generate ad revenue from mobile devices. As one *Business Insider* story asked, "Will Facebook Survive the Shift to Mobile?" Facebook was behind for legacy reasons as much as anything else. Its platform had been built by engineers most at home with software developed for the desktop, so the company initially tried to use that software to cobble together its smartphone app. The result was a slow, unstable kludge. In the spring of 2012, fewer than twenty Facebook developers were assigned to mobile. When the company went public that May, its ad revenue came entirely from ads on desktop computers.

Then Zuckerberg launched a full-scale attack on mobile. He put mobile developers on every product team. As he explained to one financial analyst, "I told all of our product teams, when they came in for reviews: 'Come in with mobile. If you come in and try to show me a desktop product, I'm going to kick you out. You have to come in and show me a mobile product.'" Instead of struggling to adapt a legacy product, Facebook's teams were unleashed to think first about creating great mobile products. New offerings emerged left and right, embodying the Facebook ethos of "move fast and break things." Many never panned out: you probably haven't spent a lot of time using Paper, Slingshot, or Rooms—to cite three flops. But many terrific ideas also flew up from the teams, and were implemented with speed and rigor. The overall result is astounding. By the end of 2016, mobile accounted for 84 percent of the company's ad revenue. Annual revenue reached $27.6 billion, up from $7.8 billion in 2013, Facebook's first full calendar year as a public company. And more than 1.15 billion people across the globe log into Facebook daily on their mobile devices, twice the number that did so in 2013.

Zuckerberg's commitment and focus were critical to the turnaround. But without the team-based culture he had built over the years, Facebook might have gone the way of other erstwhile tech powerhouses, like Netscape and Yahoo. Managing a collection of empowered teams is complicated, but Facebook does it better than almost any other company. CHRO Lori Goler, who joined Facebook in 2008, describes a culture of autonomy and initiative, where different kinds of leadership can be found at every level.

Both teams and individual employees have considerable autonomy. There's no standard way of attacking a problem—teams develop their own sensibility and process for each project. One programmer who worked on the development of Messenger, Facebook's texting app, described the team as a "startup environment" within the company: "We have the freedom to determine how to execute on our goals. With the breadth of different opportunities in Messenger (teams focused on monetization, core infra, growth, etc.) we have many different engineering and product challenges. A great number of features on Messenger have been spearheaded by an engineer with an idea. There is no limit to what you can achieve when you're passionate about what you do."

Facebook takes employee passions seriously. While some teams might last for a year or more, others disband after just a few weeks. After individual employees finish one project, they get to choose their next team. The Hackamonth program, which was spontaneously created by Facebook employees, encourages staffers to try out a new project for a month. If they like it, they can stay on the team. If they don't, they can go look for something else. The governing theory behind this, says Goler, is that employees given true autonomy will come up with solutions that make the most sense to them, rather than trying to fit their work into a construct created by some higher-up.

There's an important corollary to this empowerment of individuals across hundreds of teams: to make it work, the company needs great *managers*. It needs them to establish how team leaders and team members will be selected. It needs them to allocate funding, to keep this fluid organization moving toward a common goal, and to ensure that the company's values and behaviors are intact at the team level. It also needs great team leaders. How to find them in a company where individuals are given so much power? As one *Wall Street Journal* article explained in its headline: "At Facebook, Boss Is a Dirty Word."

Goler believes she knows how to ferret out the best managers. In her nine years at the company, she has spent a lot of time trying to understand just what management and leadership means at Facebook. To find out what characteristics marked the best team leaders, she surveyed the company's roughly twelve thousand employees and learned which teams were the most satisfied and engaged, and why. The leaders of the highest-performing teams cared about their team members, provided opportunities for career growth, set clear expectations and goals, held their teams accountable for success, and recognized outstanding performance. These are not surprising results. They fit the Management 101 description of a great manager.

But Goler gleaned another piece of data that was particularly valuable: The best managers *wanted* to be managers. The worst had moved into those roles because they believed that was the path to greater tangible rewards, like increased compensation and prestige. Organizations wedded to traditional corporate hierarchy promote their most skilled people into managerial slots as a matter of course. It's a terrible mistake that saps the passion of your company's key employees, who often move into management because of the greater financial rewards. But at Facebook, you can now keep boosting your career (and pay) without ever moving onto the managerial ladder. In fact, smart companies in a variety of industries have recognized the need for dual career tracks. Insurers Chubb and GEICO take pains to make sure that their best claims adjusters can continue to rise in stature, pay, and respect without having to move into management. "Taking your best engineer and making them a manager is not always the best approach," says Goler. "People in management should want to manage. We make it possible for people to raise their hands to become managers. And, generally, the people who raise their hands are the ones who do a good job of it."

Facebook is the perfect example of how you, as CEO, must be both visionary and grounded in the details of the talent at your company. You and your CHRO don't have to manage the day-to-day workings of all these teams. In fact, doing so would seriously undermine their independent spirit. But you do need to know when and why a team has crashed, and you must also have a great sense of who in your ranks could turn things around. That's the details part. Communicating your vision clearly is just as important. Thanks to Zuckerberg's clarity, everyone at Facebook knows where the company is headed.

Think Platform, Not Structure

If agility is the philosophical underpinning of a talent-driven enterprise, platforms are the structural foundation. In this model, traditional hierarchy gives way to a marketplace that provides talent and resources to a collection of small teams that cut across business lines and market segments. Says Susan Lund, a partner at the McKinsey Global Institute, "As the old view of hard and dotted lines begins to fade, companies might choose to group employees by their strongest activities and skills. From this functional home, they could be 'rented,' via a talent market, by business-line and project leaders." It's a move that reflects the new, permeable workplace, where your company's workforce is likely to include full-timers, part-timers, contractors, gig-economy aficionados, and, eventually, robots with artificial intelligence. A talent marketplace helps managers reallocate all these labor resources quickly when priorities and directions shift.

Perhaps the best example of this approach is Haier, China's largest home-appliance manufacturer. CEO Zhang Ruimin is a visionary leader whose goal has always been to create a company that readily provides solutions to any problem that bedevils its customers (although Haier prefers to call them "users"). That's a very different mindset from a CEO who thinks about his or her company simply as a manufacturer of products. Haier has been user focused for decades; it famously created a device to clean sweet potatoes after rural service representatives kept being called in to fix washing machines that farmers were using to prep vegetables for market.

Back in 2005, eyeing a future that seemed atypically unpredictable, Zhang set about proactively transforming Haier into a company that could react quickly to changing consumer tastes in a volatile economy. "In the Internet era," he has explained, "every company must strive to eliminate the distance between the producer and the user." To do that, Zhang radically restructured Haier by breaking down the entire organization into around two thousand micro enterprises called *zi zhu jing yi ti* (which translates to *independent operating unit,* although colloquially Haier calls each unit a "small and micro.") These small and micros are the basic innovation units of the company's new organizational grid. Each is composed of ten to twenty people drawn from a range of functions. Some stay together for years, while others disband within weeks.

The system tries to unleash the creative power of both individuals and teams by delegating decision making, personnel decisions, and resource management to each small and micro. The units are even responsible for their own P&L, which Haier calls the "win-win value-adding statement." The phrase emphasizes the fact that each small and micro serves a trio of stakeholders—the company, the user of its product, and the community that is affected. By focusing ferociously on this trio, each small and micro is expected to deliver great lifetime user value in customized, ecofriendly products. Since products are so deeply customized, payment varies as well, reflecting the specific value created by the specific small and micro. Zhang believes that this carefully balanced combination of competition and opportunities is what gets the most out of his employees. "A company that has vigor," he has said, "depends on whether the opportunities are fair, not on whether the results are fair. I have built a platform that provides equal opportunities for my employees to compete and fight for the top."

CEO Zhang hasn't just dismantled hierarchy, he's turned the very concept on its head. In most companies, product decisions are made by managers at the top of the decision chain. At Haier, users drive the product decisions, and everything else flows from their choices. As radical as they are, the small and micros are in some ways merely the logical organizational representation of a philosophy that prizes user solutions above all else.

In practice, Haier functions as a network-based, flexible system. Planning, R&D, manufacturing, marketing, and after-sales interact with users together, on a real-time basis. Business units are abandoned, formed, or adjusted based on the changing needs of users, so that Haier can adapt immediately.

People go where their individual skills are needed, regularly shifting in and out of the small and micros. Zhang uses every resource possible to ensure that a consumer trend or a technology shift never catches Haier by surprise: he insists that all seventy thousand employees interact constantly with users.

The sixty-eight-year-old Zhang, who for years has been telling employees that change is constant, is hardly finished with his organizational revolution. He is now pushing the bounds of what it means to be a company with what's being called Haier's "networking strategy." Haier shares its user data with suppliers, who are even invited on user interactions so they can see consumer needs first-hand. Users can customize their refrigerators over COSMOPlat (China's online industrial internet platform). Appliances are built with sensors, so Haier can call customers before a machine breaks down. It's an openness that sounds radical, but it's also a coolly rational acknowledgment that the internet has broken down all kinds of traditional barriers. In fact, Zhang is embracing this ethos so thoroughly that he is reportedly considering eliminating Haier's middle management.

Zhang's radical restructuring of Haier brilliantly anticipated this era of product customization and market fragmentation. Haier's revenue has grown at a 6 percent average annual rate over the past decade, while profits have soared at a 30 percent average clip. Haier is now the largest home appliance manufacturer in the world.

One final note: Haier works, and works brilliantly, despite its seeming complexity. That's in large part because Zhang believes that employees who are empowered and properly incentivized can be trusted to make the right decisions. That's an attitude that busts bureaucracy. Guess what department plays much less of a role at Haier than at most other companies? The answer is human resources. Since each small and micro manages its own P&L, demand for centralized HR services is low. The number of HR staffers at Haier has dropped dramatically over the last few years.

McKinsey itself is an example of a talent-driven company that takes the platform concept to an even greater extreme. The consultancy has 1,800 partners empowered to solve client needs. When a project is engaged, it is the partners' responsibility to assemble a team that has the necessary set of skills. Who's the functional expert? Who has the sector expertise?

Unlike at Haier, however, employees don't reside in standing performance units. Some will join a team for the full course of the assignment. Others come in only when needed. The team itself disbands after the assignment. At any one time, the company may have five thousand client projects in operation, and few are handled by teams composed of the exact same experts. The result is what McKinsey calls "a network of capabilities." It's a very talent-centric model, where enormous trust is placed in the partners, who are, in some ways, business units of one.

Make the Work Meaningful

At both Facebook and Haier, employees think "solution" before "profit." There's an assumption—which has been borne out repeatedly by the marketplace—that excelling at the former will lead naturally to the latter. The solution-first approach reflects an appropriately modern, flexible understanding of how quickly marketplace dynamics can shift, and both companies have shown an admirable ability to pivot quickly.

A solutions-first approach also forces a company to really define its mission, an exercise that almost always gives employees a greater sense of the purpose of their employer. This search for meaning in work is the third element that must be addressed by any corporate transformation.

All the reorganizing in the world won't unleash the talent inside your company if employees don't believe in the company mission. All too often, employees have seen that "purpose-driven" efforts launched from high in the organization amount to little more than flag waving. The challenge for you is to convey and live something meaningful, especially when your workforce is transient and skeptical of anything that smacks of corporate PR, as millennials especially are. Gallup has found that only 30 percent of US employees feel a strong connection to their company and work for it with passion. In fact, the same poll found that nearly 20 percent of employees consider themselves "actively disengaged." According to Gallup's CEO, this desire to find meaning in the workplace is the biggest shift he has seen in thirty years.

There are various ways you and your CHRO can counter this alienation, some of which we'll address in following chapters. The one we'll address here is a critical first step: make employees a central part of your transformation into a talent-driven organization.

In 2013 Amgen launched a reorganization that illustrates how talented, empowered employees can often design a more powerful transformation than anything you or your other colleagues in the C-suite could come up with on your own.

CEO Bob Bradway and then-CHRO Brian McNamee's biggest concern was this: Did Amgen have the skills and culture it needed to lead in an increasingly complicated business? As a first step, the two leaders convened thirty key members of Amgen's critical 2 percent. Their mission: define what Amgen needed to be over the long term, and design whatever initiatives were needed to achieve that goal.

When you ask employees what they need to succeed the answer is almost never going to be "a better strategy." The members of Amgen's thirty-person team said they wanted the biotech firm to be the most admired company by patients, and the best place for talented people to work. Working in clusters devoted to such matters as talent, customer relations, and innovation, the team developed and launched nineteen initial change initiatives.

Almost every initiative has had a significant impact on the Amgen culture. One focused on recruiting talent, a critical issue for any company drawing from a limited pool of top candidates. The talent group recommended that Amgen—which is headquartered in Thousand Oaks, California, just north of Los Angeles—go to the scientific talent rather than making the talent come to the company. As a result, the company has built up its R&D presence in Boston and San Francisco, two cities that draw some of the country's best scientists.

Another group focused on better servicing patients. Seeing where health tech was headed, it recommended that Amgen up its digital game, and fast. Initiatives were quickly launched to reduce product-development time and to improve the company's communication with patients. A slew of changes followed, including the creation of a new stand-alone digital business, which uses data to help doctors better predict how patients will fare on a variety of medications, and to help patients stay on their prescribed therapies. A collaboration with Stanford University developed complex algorithms that help physicians identify patients with very high risk of a rare cardiovascular disease.

Transparent and constant communication with the staff has been crucial to the success of Amgen's transformation. "You just don't come out and say we're going to do this to you," says McNamee. "To make sure we had everyone's support, we reached out to the broader company to explain what was happening and to make the case for change. This sounds like soft stuff, but the communication was critical to make it a credible program, and not just the latest change effort."

Communication is more than just a PR effort. Having seen that Bradway and McNamee are taking their concerns and input seriously, employees across the company have gotten involved. McNamee created a "change-agent network" of 350 people who report on the health and the risks of each initiative. The change agents report back at least once a month, more frequently when an initiative is wobbling. An initiative looking to improve communications with patients got shut down after change agents reported that the team was doing nothing more than trying to force old modes of patient communication under the banner of transformation.

When Bradway put McNamee in charge of the transformation, neither man had any idea how complex the undertaking would be. "The scale was huge," McNamee says. "It was a full-time job. I used to sit a couple doors down from the CEO, and I moved to an open workplace with my team. The CEO said he didn't plan on that. I told him, 'I'm cutting the cord and jumping out of the airplane.'" With McNamee working full time on the transition, Bradway gave him a new title—Executive Vice President of Full Potential Initiatives—and named an interim CHRO.

McNamee found it extremely useful to be a neutral player, rather than a CHRO with turf and an agenda. "I'm interacting with the CEO direct reports and saying, 'Everyone is going to have to take a risk and put everything on the table for improvement,'" he explains. "And if they are going to trust me, I've got to have a neutral agenda. If the person being the change agent is also a player, it can get in the way. Over time we were able to install a change process and common language that has evolved into a continuous improvement approach for the company."

At Amgen, the idea that change is never-ending has become a given. Employees across the company have made change a part of their job description. By 2016, more than six hundred managers were fully engaged in transformation efforts, and more than thirty company-wide initiatives had been launched. Retention metrics are rising and participation in engagement surveys is up. McNamee says the executive team now has a new problem: it is getting more new ideas than it can handle. Financial results are up. But the most telling indicator of how deeply transformation has become ingrained in the Amgen culture is this: four of the CEO's new direct reports came out of this transformation process. And McNamee has been able to return to his post as CHRO.

Amgen's successful reinvention points to the power of engaging your critical 2 percent in corporate transformation from the beginning. If you want to create a company designed to unleash talent, put the design in the hands of that very talent. And if you want to create a movement behind your transformation, start with a small group of change agents.

Tadashi Yanai is taking this approach at Fast Retailing, the Japanese company that owns brands such as Uniqlo, GU Energy, Theory, and Comptoir des Cotonniers. Yanai, a remarkably nimble CEO who has aggressively expanded overseas, believes that retailing is on the verge of a major transition. "Digital will change everything," he says. "Retail, textile, apparel industry: these are no longer real distinctions. Whoever does a good job of capturing it all will lead a new industry." Yanai knows that he can't envision this future on his own. That's why he and Noriaki Koyama, who oversees people matters, have painstakingly assembled a select cohort of Fast Retailing's critical 2 percent to begin the transition to this uncertain future.

The group Yanai selected is made up of thirty-eight young workers from all corners of the globe and all levels of the company. Most are merchandisers and marketers, but three are from HR, three from finance, and four from R&D. They are not the highest-ranking officers in the company. "To tell the truth," says Yanai, "my high-level executives are very good in the day-to-day nitty-gritty, but we need a fresh perspective. Besides, we can bring them in when we need their expertise."

As Yanai assembled the group, he looked for individuals with qualities he wants Fast Retailing to embody in the future: humility, trustworthiness, and a curious hunger for new ideas, along with the ability to listen well, spot talent, and get things done. The goal of the thirty-eight is to imagine and lead the way to a future in which Fast Retailing boosts profits by executing its core mission—making and selling clothes for the masses—in a more agile, more digitally savvy manner. But Yanai sees the transition as far more than merely adding tech chops. "A majority of our executives are left-brain oriented," says Yanai. "In the future, our business will migrate more toward right-side thinking. You can get your calculations done by a computer. That's why those with the human skills, those who are very good at capturing the holistic picture, should be the leaders of the future." To capture the potential of the digital future of retailing, Fast Retailing will have to change its very soul, starting with Yanai's handpicked group of thirty-eight.

Given those stakes, it's not surprising that Yanai is ready to do whatever it takes to support his small group of carefully chosen change makers. He's steering them through a series of exercises and assignments designed to help them learn more about the customer and the company. He deliberately arranges them into cross-functional teams, so the observations are made through the eyes of people with many different skills.

From this small core group, he expects to influence many others in the company. After their first assignment, each cross-functional team pitched an original idea for the retailer to the executive team. Yanai wants to seed the company with fresh thinking. When the thirty-eight have completed their exercises, they will take prominent roles within the company, at which point they will put their own top people through the same kind of program. One of their key responsibilities will be to spawn more such groups, with the company eventually becoming a network of networks, each built with the expectation of continuously meeting customers' changing needs. The one constant is the CEO's involvement: Yanai says that he is willing to devote

30 percent—even half—of his time to interacting with the group. "That's my job," he says. "I'm willing to build everything from scratch."

Define and Support a New Social Architecture

Teamwork. Platforms. Meaning. These are the foundational elements of any substantial reorganization taken on by a company that wants strategy to be driven by people. Each demands its full share of your attention, as does one more feature of corporate design: the social architecture of your firm.

We define social architecture as the set of norms guiding how work happens in an organization. Think of it as encompassing the ground rules for the processes and behaviors teams will use to turn ideas into value, a common vocabulary for everyone trying to work together toward a clearly understood goal. These rules should set the tone of debate and foster a mindset that supports constructive change.

We believe social architecture can be measured and monitored. Before you launch any company-wide reorg, you and your CHRO should map out the behaviors and mindsets that are most prevalent in the organization. Where are the key decision points? Who makes the final call? Does the leader allow for and fully consider points of view offered by staffers from another discipline? Are decisions made in a timely fashion? This is the nitty-gritty of your company's process; fissures here can make it impossible to rebuild the company.

Understanding the social architecture well means that you can credibly tell employees what you are really hoping to accomplish with a reorganization. Generalities like "we want to change the culture" or "we want talent to thrive" give employees little specific sense of what you are trying to accomplish. It's far better to tell employees what behaviors need to change. By communicating that your reorganization has a specific goal to correct a widely acknowledged set of problems, you garner respect at the get-go.

A clear map of the company's social architecture allows you to monitor developments throughout your reorganization. You and your CHRO should regularly check those key decision points, by sitting in on meetings where big decisions are being made. Does marketing still dominate the conversations, even though you are trying to build up the role of your company's engineers? Are the ideas of overseas participants sitting in via Skype given a real hearing, or are they drowned out by the louder opinions of the folks at headquarters? Is a certain executive's polite manner effective or off-putting? Sitting in and observing how well teams are working is the corporate equivalent of conducting an MRI. Strengths and weaknesses, missed connections, boorish behavior, and the like come to the attention of your CHRO. It is the equivalent of the CFO poring over the books to discover the need to raise cash, cut costs, or adjust the portfolio.

Finally, your CHRO should steadily analyze the corporate dynamics of your competitors and benchmark those against the behaviors that drive (or hinder) your own company's results. Companies that don't benchmark often tell themselves they excel at something like "customer focus," without having any facts to back up the assertion. McKinsey uses an approach called the Organizational Health Index (OHI) to measure the specific management practices and behaviors that define the social architecture of a company, and these measurements are benchmarked against the responses from over two million respondents at 1,500 companies. The OHI measures thirty-seven specific management practices that drive the day-to-day experience of people at these companies—in other words, the social architecture that defines how work gets done.

This kind of rigorous benchmarking is critical. Your social architecture should support and drive the talent-first organization you want to create. But it's not enough to move to talent platforms and empowerment if you don't change the day-to-day practices, behaviors, and norms that influence how work gets done. Rigorous benchmarking will make it easier for you to pinpoint the areas in your company where behavioral change is most needed. This, too, is an ongoing process—an important part of the ongoing reorganization required of a truly agile company.

Getting Started

What organizational structure will drive an explosion of talent-driven value at your company? By considering three important qualities that are shared by most talent-driven companies, you can begin to determine the approach that works best for you.

First, design your organization for agility. By agility, we mean the ability to adapt swiftly to the unpredictable trends that disrupt and reshape your industry. As you do so, keep in mind the idea that your company should nonetheless have a fixed backbone comprising the structure, processes, and governance that support dynamic teams that mobilize quickly and move freely to pursue a wide range of opportunities. Facebook offers a good model. Its people work in teams that form and disband as occasion warrants. It offers alternative career paths and compensation that directly reward value creation. Ask yourself how Facebook's processes and governance might be adapted to your company.

Second, think platform, not structure. This means replacing a fixed vertical hierarchy with an internal market that governs the deployment of talent. The examples we've offered, from Haier and McKinsey, may seem radical at first blush. But we believe that many companies in many different industries can benefit from this kind of market-driven, fluid organization. Really knowing the composition of your critical 2 percent will help you think through this organizational challenge. What structure will spark the ingenuity of your group of talented people?

The third step sounds simpler: make work meaningful. This may seem easy to dismiss, since it sounds so "soft." But you and your CHRO must address this seriously. It's not just millennials who crave purpose at work. A sterile workplace will never capture the full potential of any truly creative person. If you're not thinking this through with your CHRO, you will never attract, and keep, the great talent that you need in order to thrive in our unpredictable economy.

There's a fourth step for you as well: understand your company's social architecture, and measure and monitor it. This will be an ongoing concern, given that you're never finished designing and redesigning the organization. Having a clear map of your company's social architecture will help ensure that that architecture doesn't come apart under the pressure of constant change.

Haier CEO Zhang Ruimin once told reporters that large companies need to "lose control step-by-step." That sounds scary, but it's a keenly perceptive description of how to optimize organizations in an era of constant change. A reinvented HR department—the subject of our next chapter—will give you the on-the-ground means to manage such a fluid structure.

Make HR a Source of Competitive Advantage

For years, people have written about the need to reinvent HR. The rise of the talent-driven organization transforms that idea into an immediate imperative.

If talent is king, finding, recruiting, supporting, and developing that talent is mission-critical work. Yet many business leaders, and their employees, continue to regard human resources primarily as a back-end service, responsible only for the administration of such things as benefits packages, payroll, onboarding, and training. Those tasks are necessary. But they don't add tremendous value, which may be why some 72 percent of non-HR leaders rate the performance of HR as merely adequate, or worse.[1] The human resource department of a talent-driven organization must take on so much more. But a recent Korn Ferry study of 7,000 CHROs revealed that 83 percent of them worry that their HR organizations lack the talent to deliver on strategic priorities. As we've illustrated in previous chapters, some organizations get this—but many more do not.[2]

The time has come to fix this problem, once and for all.

In this chapter, we'll help you begin the transformation of your company's human resource department. We'll look at enlightened companies that have already begun this work, some of whom are already reaping great benefits. These companies have certain things in common. First, their talent leaders are top performers, each with meaningful experience and deep understanding of their company's business. The CHROs of such companies work closely with the CFO, because personnel and finance decisions are inextricably linked. As Hugo Bague, the former CHRO of Rio Tinto, says, "I don't see myself as an HR person. I see myself first as a business leader, who happens to focus on the people and organizational issues." Second, talent leaders add significant analytic insight to the increasing volume of data they collect about their people—and they automate or streamline processes that don't require such analysis. Third, each such company has turned its HR staff into an entrepreneurial force that adds value throughout the company. Just as important, their CEOs have made HR experience a critical part of the résumé of high-potential managers.

We recommend two additional changes to your current practice. First, we believe every business unit should have its own G3, in which the unit's HR partner takes on a significantly expanded role. Second, you'll have to back up your support of HR's bigger role with money: it's time to end the disparity between the pay of CHROs and that of the other members of the C-suite.

Unleash the Business Talent atop HR

We've already talked about the fact that your CHRO must be a star performer to justify a place in the G3. Since we are now about to look at how the two of you, together, can reinvent HR, let's revisit the qualities you need from a CHRO who can earn and command the respect of his troops and everyone at the company.

Larry Costello has been working in human resources for forty-four years, ever since he started at UPS as a part-time supervisor loading and unloading trucks at night. "The operational piece was pretty straightforward," he recalls. "The complicated part was the people." Over his time at PepsiCo, Campbell's, Trane, and Tyco, Costello established a reputation as a top-notch CHRO who was also a powerful business advisor to the CEOs he worked with. In 2015, George Oliver, then the CEO of Tyco, described Costello as "one of the most strategic thinkers of the senior management team."

Put simply, if your CHRO is not a first-rate business leader whom you can trust completely, your company's HR department will never become more than a source of administrative support. Costello draws a distinction between CHROs who are true business partners to their CEOs and those who aren't. "Most traditional HR leaders think about process and programs, and in terms of HR, they don't let themselves get engaged in strategic initiatives," he says. "They haven't invited themselves into those opportunities to be battle-tested. It's not about building out an HR department. It's about building out an HR capability. It's not about having the best health plan or comp plan. It's about being aligned with the needs of the business."

Costello has taken on all kinds of roles over his career, always from his base as an HR leader. He has stepped into operating roles, merged business divisions and territories, led projects in major overseas markets, and steered strategic planning. "To have credit as an HR leader, you have to know stuff," he says. "You have to know how to unleash human capital. You have to be willing to be engaged in the business, and have the courage to have a point of view. Most HR people don't have courage. You have to be comfortable with data. You have to get out there and actually touch people. And you have to be comfortable with the strategy. It's about influencing the strategic direction of the company."

Costello embodies the idea of a CHRO who is also a business partner, someone who has earned his or her place in a G3 and contributes mightily. We think there are at least eight characteristics to look for when assessing whether your CHRO has what you need to pull off a talent-driven reorganization:

1. Excellence in judging people and matching top performers to the jobs where they can add the most value.

2. A sixth sense for diagnosing how poorly or well an organization is functioning; a nose for pinpointing the root causes of serious problems *and* breakthrough successes; and an intuitive fairness that corrects or rewards the people involved.

3. The intellectual curiosity to search relentlessly for outside talent and compare it with your own top talent.

4. Leadership, preferably developed through assignments in line businesses as well as in HR.

5. The capacity and willingness to weigh in, as part of the G3, on capital decisions in which talent can be the difference between success and failure.

6. No desire to accumulate power for prestige or ego.

7. The courage to promote extraordinary young talent over veterans, to sustain and motivate an organization in perpetual change, to speak with candor, and to disagree heartily with you.

8. The acuity and sensitivity to work in sync with your CFO, transforming that two-person relationship into your most powerful tool.

This last one is critical if your G3 is going to work. Amgen's Brian McNamee describes the kind of conversations CHROs and CFOs should be having. "The CEO staff look at everything together," he says. "What are the improvement opportunities we are leaving on the table? Speed to market? Speed in market? The operating leaders know everything is fair game potentially, and the value is in having the team cocreate what we are going to go after and become strong sponsors for the change process." At Amgen, employees from HR do stints on the finance staff, and vice versa, so that every leader in HR or finance gets accustomed to evaluating the business from both perspectives. They work closely together designing the company's compensation packages.

Don't expect this kind of cooperation to take hold overnight, says McNamee. "Cocreating that transparency takes time. If I've learned anything about transformation, it's go slow up front to go fast later. The payoff is so great, and you will unleash energy that will exceed anything you thought the group could do. I call it the pain of cocreation—the value outstrips the pain."

As CEO, you are the linchpin of the G3. You need to foster this relationship between your two right-hand people attentively. It's essential to ensure the rapid transformation of your talent resources. "A lot of CHROs don't try to develop a relationship with the CFO, and lots of CFOs don't even think of it," says Dan Phelan, the ex-CHRO at GlaxoSmithKline. Are your CFO and CHRO presenting proposals together? Is one or the other dominant in a way that restrains honesty? Is your CHRO a financially savvy, strategic thinker? Is your CFO developing people skills? Combined, are they your most powerful tool for driving change? If not, you may need to make a change with one or both: you can promote the relationship by having them tackle important assignments together, but these are experienced leaders who aren't likely to change easily. "But," says Phelan, "if you get these two parts of the business right, chances are you're going to have a successful business."

HR Must Add Value and Insight to Data

To become a more effective and respected value creator in your company, HR must provide salient, timely information on what works and what doesn't in talent recruitment, retention, placement, and development. It must also create detailed portraits of who does what and how well a candidate or employee performs within an organization. Even more important, HR leaders need to drive talent decisions based on a deep understanding and an insightful analysis of data. Whom shall we hire? What should we pay them? How can we retain these employees and help them grow and develop as their careers progress? Such people decisions are at the crux of organizational health not only for executives but also for entry-level workers, administrative staff, sales teams, and customer-service representatives.

As discussed in prior chapters, the digital tools that HR leaders have at their disposal are expanding and improving exponentially. More than half of the 230 executives that responded to a recent Harvard Business Review Analytic Services poll said they planned to advance their HR data-analytics capacities significantly in the next few years.[3] Many CHROs have already recognized this trend, and are hiring specialists in next-gen analytics. In fact, the potential for these analytics is so great that you may want to build a data-science center—a digital center of excellence within your company— with its head reporting to the CFO and CHRO jointly. The expenditure could pay off in many ways, especially in terms of finding, assessing, monitoring, and developing talent. These digital centers of excellence, some of which already exist, are staffed by employees with skills such as data science, statistics, and AI/machine learning, who compile and analyze data to solve talent questions posed by operations managers.

For now, most of this data is backward-looking, reporting on the past performance of talent. However, we may be at the advent of the predictive-analytics era. These sophisticated analytics might expand managers' ability to find talent at all different levels of the company, diminish the chances that top performers will be assigned to unsuitable roles, and streamline such processes as corporate succession and talent development.

Companies armed with digital centers of excellence will be better-positioned to apply these more sophisticated analytics.

Leading organizations are quickly moving in this direction. PepsiCo, for example, uses analytics to address business needs. Says PepsiCo senior HR executive Shakti Jauhar, "Through innovation, we deliver analytics and actionable insights directly to our business leaders. From their mobile devices, leaders will be able to see talent trends such as turnover for their region or country and be able to act faster than ever before."

No matter how sophisticated the software becomes, though, none of this will happen without the critical human ingredient: intelligent, effective HR professionals who can turn their own analysis of the data into useful advice and actionable plans. HR's leading role in this data-rich environment is to put this information to use in developing paths, assignments, and teams that create value. But that's easier said than done—many HR departments won't be able to do this until they build new capabilities.

Historically, many HR departments have focused on hiring employees equipped for routine administrative work, often at the expense of business acumen or strategic vision. According to a recent Korn Ferry survey, 41 percent of CHROs say that business acumen is the hardest skill for them to find when hiring. But if you want an HR department that contributes far more than administrative support, you and your CHRO need employees with business savvy. Your HR staffers should be as adept at understanding the complex needs of your business as they are at understanding the needs of your complex employees.

Creating a staff filled with these kinds of strategic thinkers is likely to involve a slow and painful transformation. Many HR workers have grown up in a service culture centered around explaining benefits, salary increases, and workplace behavioral norms to company employees. It may well be that they haven't had to think strategically, to see themselves as leaders who can contribute as much value to forward-looking discussions as, say, leaders from manufacturing or marketing. Some of your existing HR people will be able, perhaps with training, to make the transition. Others will not.

CHROs of the new generation see that HR is a field where creative leaders can have real impact on the business. They are interested in the strategic side of HR, where they can marshal data to bring an external perspective on talent, sharpen talent strategy, develop leadership, and continually ensure that talent is linked to the creation of value. These are the people that you, as CEO, want throughout your HR department: creative thinkers and doers intent on making an impact on the business. They don't all have to come from the same mold. Google's former VP of people operations, Laszlo Bock, followed what he called a "three-thirds" hiring model for his HR team: One-third came from traditional HR backgrounds. One-third came from strategic consulting firms. And the last third came armed with advanced degrees in analytical fields.

Still, the reality is that, for now, your CHRO and the HR department must also continue to oversee the company's bread-and-butter personnel functions, such as payroll, policy enforcement, and benefits. As you and your CHRO reinvent HR, it's helpful to think of the department as two entities: one that focuses on strategy, spending its time trying to leverage talent into value for your company while working closely with business partners across various divisions, and one that spends its time and resources focusing on operational, transactional HR functions. Roughly speaking, the transactional tasks are payroll, the HR helpdesk, benefits administration, comp administration, and labor-law enforcement. These are all necessary and important, but they are table stakes. The strategic HR functions, on the other hand, include talent strategy, organizational diagnosis, learning and development, recruiting, performance management and compensation strategy, and the coaching and development of leaders. Each of these tasks requires strategic thinking, business training, and the sensitivity to customize plans that challenge people to keep expanding their capacity. Learning and development, for example, has sometimes been addressed with a one-size-fits-all mentality. But in a talent-first organization, learning and development must be customizable and adaptable to serve the needs of a wide range of talent working in today's fluid economy.

In far too many companies, the obligatory transactional work drains time, energy, and resources from the strategic work. That doesn't have to be the case. Working with your CHRO, you should be able to streamline the transactional side over the next few years, through a combination of process improvements, outsourcing, and automation.

In an era of smartphones and digitally savvy employees, you can generate significant savings by letting managers and employees do many of the things that HR has traditionally done. Employees can now use mobile apps to fill in job histories, skill levels, courses taken, and hours worked. This isn't as risky as it might once have been. Younger workers are more accustomed to conducting transactions online than they are to accomplishing such tasks by talking with someone face-to-face or on the phone. Allowing them to do the same within the company is merely a reflection of the times we live in, and HR should give employees more trust than it has in the past. One CHRO, who was considering the elimination of several HR-driven approval processes, was asked why HR felt the need to "police" the business. She responded, "Well, I guess we just don't trust managers." Don't put *your* trust in a CHRO who feels that way.

Outsourcing and offshoring can also help. A leading agricultural company, for example, which employed highly paid instructional designers to customize learning programs in the United States and Western Europe, discovered that certain Indian cities are filled with high-end talent in this field. The result was better capabilities at a lower cost. McKinsey, to give another example, has done something similar: it has set up HR groups in Poland, Florida, and India that provide shared services for the consulting firm's 26,000 employees across sixty countries.

Automation may well push this streamlining of HR functions even further. Next-generation technologies such as robotic process automation (RPA), smart workflows, cognitive agents, and natural language processing may have a major impact on the way most HR tasks are managed. RPA deploys a software "bot" that can manage workflow across systems, applications, templates, and data sources. For example, the onboarding process at one leading American company that makes consumer packaged goods was such a tedious, cross-functional nightmare that it could take weeks before a new employee was fully embedded in the company. RPA eliminated the delays with a bot programmed to access the company's multiple systems, follow the workflow, and write emails or initiate communications where needed. Instead of waiting for sign-off from an overworked staffer, new employees got immediate responses and prompts from the bot. This is just one example of the kind of automation that is coming. Johnson & Johnson has already automated two-thirds of the transactions—such as synchronizing address changes and posting jobs—traditionally managed by HR. PepsiCo's senior HR operations leader, Shakti Jauhar says, "Thanks to innovation in the cognitive and robotics space, we could be looking at over 20 percent cost reduction in HR operations' back-office processes by driving efficiency and working in more constructive ways. Say you have a repetitive process to compile data from ten different sources; bots could do this in seconds rather than days. This would allow team members to avoid the manual work that is required to check data or process transactions—allowing them to focus on more strategic priorities."

In fact, we expect the streamlining of the transactional side of HR to progress so quickly that you could even split that side off entirely from HR, creating one shared service function that could report to the CFO or COO, since the focus is on managing for efficiency. The solution that's right for you depends on the nature of your company.

One thing's for certain: streamlining the transactional side of HR *without* investing in the strategic side is a recipe for disaster. Tech investments driven solely by cost reduction are a cop-out, not a strategy. As we'll see in the next section, a talent-first company needs strategic HR personnel woven into all parts of the organization. *That's* what the streamlining of HR operations should finance.

The New HR Career Path

Gleaning insights about talent from data is important. So is translating those insights into action. In today's companies, that's the job of the HR business partner, a liaison between business managers and HR. But as we've mentioned before, there is considerable evidence that HR, despite its best efforts, often falls short in this critical role.

To stock your HR department with people who can develop the skills and clout to truly add value to the business, you must reinvent the HR career track. The ideal HR partner displays intellectual curiosity, possesses a deep knowledge of the business and a feel for how it makes money, has insight when judging people, and shows a willingness to be engaged in the business and the courage to have a point of view. What can you do to attract this kind of talent to HR?

Many HR groups have tried and failed to source talent from elsewhere in the business or from different academic disciplines. The call for HR to get "closer to the business" has been a mantra for over twenty years, but has amounted to little practical change in many companies. Most HR business partners have grown up in HR roles, often starting from quite junior positions. Indeed, many of them have spent most, or all, of their professional careers in roles that are rewarded for great customer service—saying yes to requests and smoothing out wrinkles in the HR process.

You need to develop a new talent pipeline, one that delivers people with a greater diversity of experience and more exposure to the strategic levers of the business. The best way to get started is to steer HR leaders into stints in operations, and for business leaders to spend time in human resources.

Sharing of talent between HR and other parts of the business can't simply be an HR initiative—it must be your initiative as CEO, announced by you with the full backing of the board and your top management. It's an initiative that will take time, commitment, and follow-through on your part, because it will be greeted with skepticism—as we've said, your employees have heard about the "reinvention of HR" before. You and your CHRO must also make clear the personal rewards that will accompany this shift. Anyone who expects to have a senior HR position in your talent-driven company should gain experience in line jobs and in functions such as finance, to build better business-strategy capabilities. Line managers intent on becoming senior leaders should see stints in HR as a normal part of their career path.

Tim Huval, the CHRO of Humana, recognized the need for exactly this type of DNA shift in his HR organization. He wanted HR staffers to have a broader perspective, so they could clearly see the impact of their talent recommendations on the bottom line and on the future of the business. He wanted to create a culture where HR was not in conflict with where the business was headed. "I don't think of HR as a support organization," says Huval. "HR today is as much of a business and enterprise function as any other. That may sound crazy, but I actually believe that." He himself had held direct operating jobs at Bank of America before taking the HR job at Humana.

With the full backing of CEO Bruce Broussard, Huval started moving talent in and out of HR. Says Huval: "It's critical to move people into different roles where they can learn new skills if the company is going to create capabilities for the future." Huval didn't launch a formal program. Instead, he made clear that a move into operations, or other functions that directly supported operations, was voluntary—but that anyone who wanted to be a better-balanced HR leader would benefit from those experiences. One key lesson that he learned: it helps to tell any HR person thinking of getting experience outside of HR that he or she goes with an implied round-trip ticket. This provides critical peace of mind, because it gives each person the freedom to decide whether to return to HR or start a new career in another part of the business.

From the start of 2013 through mid-2017, Humana moved more than 130 HR employees (upward of 20 percent of the total HR staff) into operations and other jobs outside of HR. We spoke to one of those leaders, an IT staffing manager named Angela. She moved into Medicare quality, where the company manages relationships with physicians and physician groups to deliver quality outcomes for its members. Angela worked there for about a year, developing skills such as project management and relationship development, before returning to HR as an HR business partner.

Angela says working in provider services gave her a new perspective on HR, including the critical role of staffing for the front line. She thinks more strategically now. In one instance, she noticed that some macro trends were posing risks to associates who needed visa sponsorship, and spurred a change in the company's existing practices. Pulling from her experience in the business, she looked at this problem as a business case and tried to determine the true value not only for the IT department but also for the larger Humana enterprise. "Having been in the business, I now think from a business leader's point of view, [about] how to translate HR value into business value. I also think beyond just my vertical team, and look across the system. So, it's less around making sure I've met my objectives, and much more about having a better understanding of what this leader needs to create the best end value for their business, as well as Humana." Angela's leader, VP of HR Roger Cude, sees the change. "She now pushes back on the managers about the skills and chemistry they need in order to get the most out of their human capital," says Cude. "By taking on a job directly supporting our physicians, Angela developed a new set of skills and a more sophisticated sense of what it takes to be a great HR partner."

Huval wasn't just moving HR employees into operations. He was also moving managers from operations groups into HR for temporary stints. One of the biggest benefits of rotating line managers in and out of HR is that it gives them a new perspective on the world of human capital and how important it is to what they do day in and day out. In other words, the experience gives Humana's leaders a deeper appreciation of the importance of hiring the right people. It also helps them better understand the rhythm and a cycle of HR around such things as performance goals, evaluations, and cultural development. Since the beginning of 2016 through mid-2017, more than twenty associates have moved from the business segments into HR, slightly less than 5 percent of the total HR team.

Exposure to other parts of the company gives HR business partners a greater understanding of what it really takes for talent to succeed. It also deepens the quality of their analytics-driven insights, and improves their chances of turning those insights into real solutions. Tearing down the silo between HR and other parts of your company will reshape HR in ways you can't anticipate. For instance, consider how PepsiCo's Shakti Jauhar describes the kind of talent he seeks. "My ideal HR operations recruit has a much different profile than it did just a few years ago. Today, I look for an engineering background or a proven data analytics individual with project management experience. In my personal opinion, stocking your HR department with people like that would digitally transform HR at any company."

Huval's two-way street, with leaders from the outside coming in to HR and HR people going to different departments, is part of redefining the HR career track. But attracting the best talent to HR will take more than that. We think HR departments need to reinvent the HR business-partner job. It can't simply be about offering advice to the business units and dealing with personnel issues as they arise. That model is not going to attract the level of leadership talent that wants to feel integral to the operations of the company. Just as important, it's not what a talent-driven company needs from HR.

Create Talent Value Leaders

In a talent-driven company, the advisory business-partner role should be replaced by one in which someone can drive strategic talent decisions. It's about action, not counseling. We call the person to fill this new role the talent value leader (TVL).

We believe that every unit of the organization should have its own G3, consisting of at least the head of the business unit, the finance director, and the TVL. Just as finance "owns" the P&L, HR should "own" the talent. This means that the TVL should be held accountable for the performance of the talent in the business unit and for the organization's smooth functioning. But it also means that the TVL, unlike most of today's HR business partners, would have real clout when it comes to talent decisions.

This doesn't mean that TVLs would make the final decisions. Choosing whom to hire or fire remains the decision of the business leader or manager (as do final spending decisions, which aren't dictated by finance). But the TVL would have strong influence over how those decisions are made, and therefore would be held accountable. The TVL's performance would be judged according to the performance of talent. Metrics like engagement, attrition, gaps in critical capabilities, year-to-year development of skills, and others would be part of the evaluation of any TVL, as would the overall performance of the unit.

It's important that the TVL not get weighed down by day-to-day HR operations. If TVLs are continually forced to resolve benefit and compensation issues, they will never be able to influence strategy and talent at the business-unit level. TVLs won't succeed if the managers in the business units don't have access to automated systems that deliver digital talent insights. Automating the information needed to make talent decisions will free up TVLs to spend more time on nurturing critical roles and shaping overall talent policies in the business units.

In some ways, TVLs are the linchpin of a talent-driven company. Their role touches on so much of what we've covered in this book. They must be keen enough to successfully shape the small teams of talent that drive your company's strategy. They must be nimble enough to perform that role in a company that is constantly reoptimizing its structure, and they must have the data and insight to know how such constant change will affect key talent. They must have the personal skills to customize training and career paths for a wide range of talent. They must be aggressive, knowledgeable recruiters with the strength of character to champion and place those valuable employees whose skills don't fit into a neat slot. The TVL plays the role you wish your HR business partners were playing today. Offering real control over a major expense category, the TVL position could attract high performers from the rest of the business as well as high potentials from universities and other pipeline sources. A fleet of TVLs executing at a high level across the company could ensure the success of your talent-driven organization. The TVL exemplifies what HR should be in the twenty-first century.

End the CHRO Pay Disparity

If HR can transform itself in the way we've described in this chapter, it will have earned a place at the executive table, and your CHRO will have earned his place in the G3. This brings us to one final observation about the place of HR in your company.

We asked Korn Ferry's Hay Group researchers to review CHRO and CFO pay data from companies with between $5 billion and $20 billion in annual revenue. After reviewing the data, Irv Becker, who heads up Korn Ferry's North American executive-pay and -governance practice, told us that, "It is clear

FIGURE 4-1

Median compensation: CFO versus CHRO

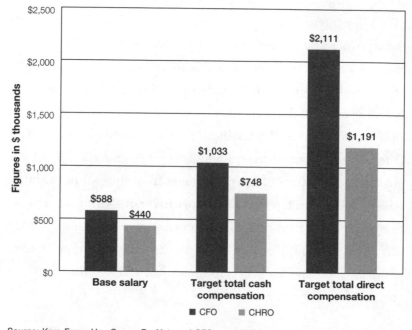

Source: Korn Ferry, Hay Group, PayNet; and CFOs and CHROs within all organizations between $5 billion and $20 billion in revenues.

that CHROs are undervalued, and are consistently paid at a discount to CFOs. The numbers range, but are typically around 50 percent or 60 percent of CFO total direct compensation in similarly sized companies." See figure 4-1 for a summary of his findings. Becker goes on to say, "This pay disparity can make a CHRO role less attractive for high-performing line managers. It can also create too wide a disparity for CHROs to be considered in the context of CEO succession."

You should help your board's compensation committee see that this situation is changing. As more line people move into HR to have a shot at becoming CEO, the level of pay in HR must become more attractive. A CHRO who adds the kind of value we've been describing should receive a compensation package comparable to that of the CFO. If that person goes unrecognized and unrewarded, she will soon move to a company that promises to treat her differently.

Less than a handful of CEOs in the *Fortune* 500 are former CHROs. The exceptions have been notable, like Mary Barra, CEO of General Motors; Anne Mulcahy, Xerox's CEO from 2001 to 2009; and Harald Krueger, who did a long stint in HR before becoming CEO of BMW. Michigan professor Dave Ulrich and Korn Ferry reviewed old assessments the recruiting firm had done of C-suite candidates, examining the way the assessments characterized each candidate's leadership style, thinking style, and emotional competency. What they found was that except for the COO (whose role and responsibilities often overlap with the CEO's), the executive whose traits were most similar to those of the CEO was the CHRO. "This finding is very counterintuitive—nobody would have predicted it," Ulrich says.

If your CHRO truly excels at linking talent and numbers, she should be a candidate to succeed you. That may sound like a stretch, given HR's historical place in the pecking order. But in a time when talent drives value more than anything else, it might make good sense. You want as CEO a person who "owns" talent as well as she understands the business. If that describes your CHRO, she deserves a shot to succeed you. At the very least, any CHRO who is helping steer the company alongside the CEO and CFO deserves to be compensated at a higher rate than 50 percent of what a good CFO commands.

Getting Started

Reinventing HR begins at the top. To unlock the potential of this perennially undervalued resource, you will have to work hand-in-hand with a CHRO you fully trust and respect as a business partner.

You and your CHRO must be able to answer two questions. Does your HR department have the technological firepower it needs? And does your HR department have the intellectual strength to add insight to the data that HR software puts at your fingertips? As we've already discussed, HR software has become truly valuable in the past few years. It is starting to have predictive capabilities that can markedly improve your ability to manage top performers and shape their career paths. But you must ensure that your HR is equipped to make the most of its power. Many people in HR have been hired and promoted for their ability to execute important administrative tasks professionally. That's not enough these days. Refocusing the staff and training its members to develop new skills will go a long way, but you and your CHRO will have to do whatever it takes to make the HR department as valuable as any other department in the company.

With a crack staff in place, you can start making moves to spread a talent-first sensibility throughout the company. We believe that every business unit in the company should have its own G3, consisting of the unit leader, the chief financial person, and a talent value leader (TVL) from HR. The TVL should have greater strategic input than HR business partners had in the past—in fact, the position of the TVL within the business unit should be as powerful as your CHRO's position in the G3.

You'll also have to reinvent the career track of your top HR talent. You'll need to groom the department's top performers in other parts of the organization, so they'll develop the business sense they'll need to contribute in their increasingly mission-critical positions. This goes the other way as well. Your high-potential leaders from outside the department should expect a stint in HR as part of their career trajectory.

Only you can lead this reinvention of HR. The minute you delegate it to your CHRO so you can "focus on more-important things" is the minute you've torpedoed your effort. A true reinvention of HR is made harder by the fact that so many people have seen a parade of weak HR initiatives come and go. Only you can convince your people that *this* reinvention of HR is the one that counts, the one that once and for all turns HR into the recruiting, developing, integrating, value-creating force that it naturally should be at every talent-first company. That's the kind of HR department you need in order to continually scale the talent and potential of your people, as you'll see in chapter 5.

Unleash Individual Talent

As we've seen, forward-looking companies will reorganize to create an environment in which talent excels. But they don't stop there. Using a variety of new technologies, they customize training, compensation, and career paths to fit the needs of their most talented employees. One-size-fits-all people planning won't work at talent-driven companies. Instead, you must individualize your approach to talent development just as rigorously as you personalize offerings to your most important customers. If your company's fate depends on talent, there's nothing more important than developing your future leaders and value creators. So, while the CHRO is a principal architect of your people processes, talent development is now one of the core responsibilities of any successful CEO.

In this chapter, we'll look at what it takes to holistically scale talent. When evaluating and deploying your best workers, you should be armed with great data that your best executives can then leverage along with their instinct and judgment. You'll need a system that's constantly in motion, supporting individuals' development in ways that align with the company direction. Whether or not you're a fan of annual reviews (which we'll address directly later in the chapter) you should be wary of the static philosophy behind them. Scaling individual talent isn't a once-a-year program; it's a never-ending, never-completed process best supported by ongoing feedback. The goal is to foster a workforce that is constantly adapting, improving, and increasing value. Executed properly, talent development will transform your employees into a "talent force"—value creators who can lead you and your company to unknown heights.

Practically, there are three steps you'll need to take to start effectively scaling up the skills of your people. First, make use of data analytics and new software to calibrate top talent and assign it to jobs where its skills can multiply value. Second, reexamine any part of talent development that's seen as a once-a-year HR function, and consider replacing or augmenting it with something that delivers continuous, enlightening feedback. In this chapter, we'll look at annual performance reviews, career paths, and pay scales. These legacy processes need to be modernized and customized to reflect the diversity of your talent and to reward agility, creativity, and results. Third, revamp your systems to keep everyone in your company learning and updating their skills.

None of these moves is sufficient on its own. But they are critical steps on the path to the creation of a talent-driven organization that engages, empowers, and unleashes your people. That's what the world's largest asset manager, BlackRock, has already done. Before taking you deeply into the three steps you need to take, let's first dive into BlackRock's unique talent-development system.

How BlackRock Makes Talent Development a Competitive Advantage

For years now, BlackRock founder and CEO Larry Fink has believed that spotting and developing the best possible talent is the key to his company's long-term success. Other CEOs say similar things, but few have demonstrated as much prescience and follow-through as Fink. Under Fink, BlackRock applies as much care and rigor to selecting its leaders as it does to picking its investments. Its heavily systematized approach to talent development ensures that talent decisions at every level of the company are grounded in a combination of smart judgment and empirical data. The result is a workplace where leadership knows it has deployed talent as well as it can, and where talent knows it has support and transparency from above.

BlackRock has the kind of alignment at the top that we've advocated in previous chapters. In its case, CEO Fink and CHRO Jeff Smith work very closely with the board of directors on talent. They typically include significant talent topics at every board meeting, and engage directors in a day-and-a-half-long deep dive on talent every year. The company's equivalent of the G3 is a G6 (consisting of the CHRO, the COO, the CFO, and the head of strategy, who lead the quarterly business review process, and the CEO and the president.) This group meets every quarter with each of BlackRock's top thirty-five business heads to review progress against financial targets, business objectives, strategic initiatives, and talent and diversity objectives, all tailored to the most critical drivers of performance in those businesses. The firm's talent strategy is driven by HR arm-in-arm with the global executive committee and a forty-six-member group known as the human capital committee (HCC). Says Smith, "I'm proud of the partnerships we have developed to integrate talent into all of our most critical business processes. This has also helped us attract and build one of the best HR teams in the world."

The HCC was formed after BlackRock's 2009 merger with Barclays Global Investors (BGI)—at the time the biggest ETF provider in the world. Fink and CHRO Smith (who had come over from BGI) originally created it to manage the cultural integration of BGI and BlackRock. It did that so well that Fink and Smith decided to keep the HCC together as BlackRock's talent leadership team. In the words of Chief Talent Officer Matt Breitfelder, the HCC is "a collection of heavyweight leaders" drawn from across the company, including senior investors, technologists, the heads of many of BlackRock's largest and most critical growth businesses, HR leaders, and others, who typically serve for two to three years. Until early 2017, Smith led the group with Vice Chairman Ken Wilson, a sage Wall Street veteran. "It's highly unusual for a person of Wilson's stature to focus almost entirely on talent and to directly mentor many of our best up-and-coming leaders," Smith says.

The HCC is at the core of all of BlackRock's talent efforts, from company-wide culture initiatives to building the pipeline of future leaders. At every stage, on almost all decisions, members mesh data analytics with observations to triangulate judgments on everything having to do with talent: performance management, leadership development, inclusion and diversity, innovation, culture, recruiting, internal mobility, career tracks, and more. For instance, when BlackRock launched a sponsorship initiative for women leaders at the company, the HCC played a central role in designing the program, tracking progress, and ensuring maximum impact. The HCC dug into the ensuing annual employee survey and found that women who were in the program expressed greater job satisfaction and garnered more promotions and other career advancements than women who weren't in the program—and that women in the program were actually more satisfied in their jobs than their male counterparts.

The annual survey of employees is BlackRock's most critical talent data-collection process. Carefully designed each year by data scientists on the HR team in partnership with HCC sponsors, it aims to identify critical areas in need of attention—in everything from processes to knowledge bases. Over the years, data has shown that employees wanted more one-on-one time and feedback from their managers, that user technology needed to be upgraded, and that employees were looking for more learning opportunities for career advancement. The HR team and HCC launched initiatives to address each problem. Just as important, the aggregate survey results (which are blinded, of course) are made available to all employees, which helps make clear that the talent initiatives were taken in direct response to their survey responses. This radical transparency is a model for any people-first company. If you say that talent will lead the company into the future, you must show that you trust that talent. Trust leads to engagement: last year, 97 percent of Black-Rock's employees completed the annual survey. Cameron Leax, head of performance and culture, says, "Our employees see a tight linkage between their feedback and positive changes in the company. And over time we expect our talent analytics to give us greater insights in predicting how employees will respond to future process changes and initiatives."

In its work on talent, BlackRock aims to emulate a shrewd investor who tries to balance gut instinct and hard data. When looking at the career development of high-potential people, the firm considers data on business unit performance and talent development. That's commonplace. But BlackRock also assesses leaders' entrepreneurialism, sense of purpose, emotional investment in the company, and ability to create new leaders on their teams. Says Breitfelder, "By design, we create some social pressure in the organization by asking our managers, 'Yeah, you think of yourself as a leader, but what's your track record? Name the people that you've developed.' We call it positive paranoia. The cultural norm is to constantly challenge people to see what they can *really* do. We want them looking in the mirror, and we want them always getting the feedback they need to get better."

Smith and Breitfelder, along with the GEC and HCC, continually review how—and how well—BlackRock is deploying its talent. It's an organizational imperative that sets an example for everyone at the company. People at BlackRock are constantly reassessing themselves. They examine their personal skill set, to be sure they're ready for the next challenge. They look at how the performance of their business unit supports the goals of the whole company. They measure themselves against the four BlackRock principles, a set of common values forged in 2012 by an HCC initiative that involved over four hundred people at the firm. This constant self-assessment isn't withering, though, since the company provides a wide range of development and mentorship opportunities.

In the previous chapter, we looked at the way talent-first organizations must continually reorganize and reinvent themselves. BlackRock's unique approach to managing talent enables continuous reinvention—both for the company and for individual employees. It's a unique system that powers itself. Every employee is asked to identify their top three areas of improvement, and the firm itself sets an annual talent and diversity agenda comprised of its top three focus areas for the firm. The more employees experience the power of progress against those goals, the more those employees are fully engaged and achieving higher levels of performance. The more the system develops strong leaders, the more those leaders will create new leaders. Says Breitfelder, "The most important thing to Larry [Fink] is that his culture can thrive for decades and that the next generation of leaders at BlackRock are doing the right things to lead the firm into the future."

BlackRock offers a great model of a complete talent development system informed by a talent-driven philosophy that is firmly rooted in the business. Any company that truly wants to scale its individual talent should embrace BlackRock's central premises: that talent development is a critical driver of value creation and performance, and that it is a never-ending process that requires the complete commitment and participation of top management. It's hard to argue with the results: after the Barclays merger, BlackRock had $2.7 trillion of assets under management. It has doubled that figure in just six years.

Now let's look at each of the individual building blocks introduced at the beginning of the chapter.

Use Software and Data to Get Your Top People into the Critical Jobs

Matching people to jobs where they can flourish energizes the organization. This is true for everyone across the organization. But it's especially true with your critical 2 percent. For each of these high-potential people, you must constantly ask the following questions: Is he or she in the right job? Is he or she in a job that allows him or her to create exponential value? Is he or she developing the skills and judgment that will be needed in the years ahead? Is he or she growing as a leader *and* creating new leaders? As we've discussed already, the care, maintenance, and monitoring of your critical 2 percent are perhaps your most important tasks as CEO. You are the gardener of talent. If the seeds you plant don't flower, your garden won't grow, and another gardener will be brought in. It's that simple.

Like BlackRock, forward-looking companies rely on next-generation analytic software, buttressed by a healthy dose of gut instinct, to allocate their top talent. Some CEOs we know dismiss the importance of this software. If you too are a skeptic, ask yourself a few questions about how promotions and transfers are handled now at your company: Are you 100 percent confident that HR always has the best and most up-to-date information about key talent throughout the company? If not, how can you be sure that managers and HR aren't overlooking good fits for important positions? Are you sure that your top talent is constantly steered toward challenging jobs that create the most possible value for the company? Is your company as rigorous about talent management as BlackRock? If the answer to any of these questions is no—as we suspect is the case for many companies—it's time for the G3 to call in the CIO and begin the process of making analytics software a powerful tool for putting the right people in the right jobs at your company. According to one recent survey of nearly three thousand business executives, managers, and analysts around the world, top-performing organizations employ analytics five times as much as lower-performing organizations do.

We are in the early stages of a revolution that will have as much impact as when Lotus 1-2-3 was introduced in the 1980s and finance departments started doing real economic analysis at scale. Companies now have real data at their fingertips on which to base decisions around human capital. As you'll see from the examples that follow, these tools will help leadership teams apply the same discipline to talent allocation that they do to capital allocation.

Clustree, a French startup, makes a program that broadens your pool of candidates. Media giant Canal+, Italian oil and gas giant ENI, and the mobile-phone provider Orange use its cloud software, which accumulates résumés and other publicly available work-history information about a company's employees. Armed with this kind of information, a CHRO can cast a wider internal net when filling a job. The software might reveal, for example, that a marketing executive has trained herself in exactly the kind of technical expertise needed for a job in manufacturing. As Clustree CEO Bénédicte de Raphélis Soissan explains, "We want to break traditional career paths."

The new software applications mine all kinds of data to improve your company's talent-spotting skills. For example, VoloMetrix, the startup Microsoft acquired in 2015 for more than $200 million, uses email data to look at productivity. It measures, say, how much time an employee spends writing emails compared with how many he or she receives. While Volo-Metrix doesn't see the content of emails, it does look at connections—who an employee is emailing and how many times a day. Seeing this kind of social-network trend can help a CHRO find employees with high potential. Let's say, for example, that one team leader spends a lot of time exchanging emails with someone higher up in the organization and outside his discipline. That may be a sign that this employee is well connected, and respected beyond his principal domain. Of course, the data alone isn't conclusive: HR execs will have to follow up by looking at performance reviews and other information. But without the software, this potential star might have gone unnoticed.

Predictive analytics software doesn't replace commonsense judgment; it supplements and improves it. A startup called HireVu, for example, has an algorithm that analyzes the video interviews of job applicants for telling personality traits. Entelo, in San Francisco, says it can discern from job applicants' online tendencies whether those applicants are likely to stick. Koru is a four-year-old company that learns the culture of your company and then designs surveys to find applicants who would fit well within that culture.

McKinsey itself worked with Oblong, a California-based developer of user interfaces, to build a program that clearly shows how this mix of data analysis and judgment works in practice. The two companies developed a tech-enabled "talent war room," where companies can put lots of different information about leaders up on multiple screens in an immersive room to rigorously consider how different personnel arrays or succession plans might play out. The system lets you go deep into the profiles of individual leaders to see their backgrounds, strengths, skill sets, and networks. It even helps identify potential candidates for critical roles using criteria that can be adjusted on the fly. The Oblong tool is multidimensional. While it helps executives decide who might be the right person for a particular job, it also helps them understand the ramifications of that decision throughout the organization. This can reduce the unintended consequences of a promotion or a transfer—consequences that are, of course, terribly hard for HR to predict. McKinsey uses the Oblong system to help clients, but also uses it internally. The consulting firm is built around small teams that assemble and disband in quick succession while tackling a variety of client assignments. The better it can assess how its teams might work together, the better its success rate will be.

To make the most of such insights, you'll have to embed data analytics in all people processes. What do we mean by embed? In a typical HR organization today, most decisions about people either implicitly or explicitly follow a process map—some steps are completed by business partners or generalists, while others are completed by HR, and still others by digital specialists. Many of these steps require a person to apply judgment and make a recommendation or a decision, such as how to evaluate an employee's performance or whom to designate as an executive's successor. Embedded analytics can inform or even replace these steps with algorithms that provide insights based on the data.

As an example, consider how succession planning is typically handled. HR probably lays out a process for the organization, designing the tools or templates to use and training key stakeholders in the process. From there, managers sit down with their HR partners to discuss potential succession candidates for key positions. While this conversation is about skills, competencies, and development pathways, the data is often incomplete. HR might then create individual development plans for potential candidates, considering the skills needed to fill the role successfully. As vacancies occur, HR and the managers meet to go over the data once more. Or they don't meet. Whether because of time pressure or distrust of the quality of the information, many managers don't take advantage of such ad hoc systems.

A succession-planning process that includes data would look and feel very different, and would drive a different outcome. First, machine-learning algorithms could review years of succession data to understand the success factors for each role, and use those insights to help identify the top five internal candidates. These recommendations could be attached to each candidate's job record, and managers could review and contact potential successors. Software analysis of each candidate's competencies would also create customized development plans based on an individual's career path. All this information could then be used in multiple ways: for one-on-one consultations between managers and strategic HR partners, for regular assessments of cross-functional bench strength, and for making sure the enterprise has the right talent to execute its strategy.

Done right, personnel analytics can radically improve your chances of getting the right people into the right jobs, scaling their talents and multiplying the value created for your company, and can reduce any unconscious bias that inhibits diversity. Getting to this level of analytics capability requires substantial investment. This isn't simply a matter of buying off-the-shelf software and plugging it in. Organizations will need to hire tech wizards who can whip into shape conflicting hardware and software systems that will be hard-put to keep up with the complex, team-based networks of talent-driven companies. But the work and investment will pay off.

Rethink Reviews, Compensation, and Other Static Processes

Many employees dread their annual review, at least in its current format. A YouGov poll of three thousand British workers discovered that one in five of them believed that their bosses didn't even think about the review until the bosses had them face-to-face in a room. A third of the respondents described the exercise as pointless. They often complained about dishonest feedback from bosses who didn't follow up on their concerns. Perhaps what they considered "dishonest" feedback was just confused feedback. In another study, researchers asked managers who share oversight of certain employees to rate those people on a scale of one to seven. "In the vast majority of cases," says RJ Heckman of the recruiting firm Korn Ferry, "the two managers disagreed about the person's performance. If one said seven, the other said below a four or a five. There was shocking disagreement on very basic areas." No wonder that 58 percent of the executives responding to a recent Deloitte survey believed that their company's current approach to performance management did absolutely nothing to drive engagement or performance. Despite this, a mere 6 percent of *Fortune* 500 companies have moved away from the annual review.

Perhaps it's unfair of us to single out the annual review. If annual reviews are handled with compassion, clarity, and solid data, and if they are part of a comprehensive program of steady feedback and training, they can be useful. But we are shining a spotlight on them to make an important point: to successfully steer a talent-driven company, you must reconsider every piece of talent-facing bureaucracy that has accreted over the years. Habits that made sense decades ago may have locked you in to ways of developing talent that no longer make sense.

As the survey data suggests, the annual review is a good place to start. Some notable forward-looking companies have eliminated annual reviews, including GE, Microsoft, and Netflix. Netflix's rationale is telling: CEO Reed Hastings thinks it makes no sense to measure people against annual objectives when his company's strategies often change at a much more rapid pace. Indeed, most of the companies we spoke to for this book are experimenting with new performance-management systems that reflect Hastings's view. The goal is to deliver more-effective feedback, often drawn from multiple sources, far more often than once a year. Again, technology is a critical tool in making this happen.

Zalando, Europe's leading online fashion platform, is currently implementing a real-time tool that crowdsources performance feedback from different touchpoints employees have with each other. After meetings, collaborative projects, and other interactions, employees give and also proactively request feedback from supervisors, colleagues, and internal customers through an online app that lets people provide both positive and critical comments in an intuitive and engaging way. Since the data is collected in real time, it tends to be more accurate than data collected at the time of annual reviews, when colleagues and supervisors must strain to remember details about past performance. Armed with swift and meaningful feedback, employees can adjust on the fly. Zalando also uses the tool to improve its ability to correlate performance and talent development.

In 2013 and 2014, Cardinal Health's then-CHRO Carole Watkins conducted a fascinating experiment to find out what kind of feedback employees really want. Cardinal, a *Fortune* 50 company with 37,300 employees who help health-care providers serve patients efficiently, relied for years on a traditional five-point rating system that determined an employee's prospect for promotion and his bonus. "Over the years, we saw a growing level of dissatisfaction with the system," says Watkins. "A rating of 'three' deflates people, and most people are rated 'three.'"

Watson created four test groups of employees and managers. One group used the traditional five-point rating system. Another adopted a three-point system. A third group relied instead on a simplified review form. And the fourth group ditched numerical ratings for quarterly coaching conversations and training. "Our theory," says Watkins, speaking of the fourth group, "was that if conversations mattered most, people would feel better about and get more out of having more conversations." The conversations were designed to be objective and unthreatening, based on known facts about the employee. A team leader might say: "It seems like you have turnover on your team. What can I do to help?" The employee was also encouraged to ask questions such as: "How do I get more exposure to senior leaders, or How do I get to the next step in my career?"

At the end of two years, members of the fourth group were 16 percent more satisfied with their jobs than those in any other group. Watson took the next step, and started rolling out the quarterly, unrated, conversation model across the company. Two thousand managers at the director level and above received feedback in this fashion in 2015. In 2016, they began teaching the method to their direct reports.

Continuing feedback works best when employees are participants in a process rather than simply receiving criticism or ratings. GE, a company once famed for its forced ranking approach, has blown up its annual reviews system and has switched to a process of continual feedback and coaching—and has replaced individual ratings, which tended to encourage a focus on past performance, with forward-focused conversations about customer priorities, employee contributions, and continuous improvement. The GE example shows how reconsidering a single process like the annual review can lead to a comprehensive rethink of how you manage talent.

Since 2008, GE has been rethinking what it means to be a leader in today's economy: "We, along with many other companies, were forced to think differently. But it wasn't just about the financial crisis. It was that we finally were beginning to see greater potential in the global changes and the virtual changes brought on by technology." GE's operating rhythm was accelerating, and the leadership tools the company had employed for decades needed to change to reflect that modern workplace.

One process that wasn't working any more was the company's annual talent-review system, a time-intensive process for assessing leadership in every business unit. Known as the EMS, or Employee Management System, this process had been devised in the 1970s and leveraged consistently since then. CHRO Susan Peters wanted something radically different, something that benefitted from technology and wasn't static in any way. "People, especially the millennials," Peters recalls, "wanted their feedback more frequently and more tied to a specific project." The replacement approach that she launched, known as Performance Development at GE, has been rolled out to all of GE's two hundred thousand salaried employees after a two-year implementation and several test-and-improve cycles with thousands of associates. Performance Development replaces a static, one-time event with a real-time, iterative process.

In GE's case, an ongoing dialogue between employees is at the heart of the program. That dialogue is facilitated by (but not exclusive to) an interactive app called PD@GE, which was developed in-house and is constantly honed as the team learns more. Says Peters: "We keep a mentality that nothing gets frozen, that nothing is, 'This is the only way to do it.'" That philosophy applies to the whole approach, not just the app. Leaders comment regularly on the performance of their team members; team members give steady feedback to each other and to their leader. Performance priorities can be updated regularly, in step with changing customer needs, and team leaders can use the system to quickly assess whether employees have the right skills and focus for the new task. The results of this 360-degree, multidimensional process are aggregated automatically, giving top executives a much better view into the day-to-day performance and leadership of their talent. At the end of the year, a summary "touchpoint" conversation between employee and manager, and a summary document which draws on insights and data from the app, make it easy to reflect on achievements and, even more important, to identify future opportunities to develop and contribute.

Performance Development at GE may be fluid and iterative, but that doesn't mean it has no guidelines or rules. Peters asked that employees deliver feedback as either a "continue" or "consider" insight. For example, a manager using the Insights app on his phone might type, "Laura, I'd like you to consider speaking up more in the meetings," a more constructive approach than, say, "Laura, you're not speaking up at meetings and that's a real problem." Taking the threat out of the advice encourages managers to use the system more and helps motivate team members. Says Peters: "The wonderful thing about positive coaching, as research shows, is that people can lean into the things that they're already good at, and do even better." Or, as the late management guru, Peter Drucker, once said: "The task of leadership is to create an alignment of strengths in ways that make weaknesses irrelevant."

GE's Performance Development system creates better feedback, drives more productive conversations between employees and leaders, and among peers, and aggregates more relevant data for executives planning strategies and career paths—and does so more efficiently than an approach GE applied for decades. That's a pretty good model for a leader who wants to make the most of his or her very best talent. The annual review isn't dead, but you need to ensure it is part of a feedback system that's as flexible as today's workforce.

Digging into your company's processes at this level isn't micromanaging—it's removing impediments that can slow your company's transition to a talent-driven organization. Processes that remain unaltered for years for no good reason have negative ripple effects throughout the organization. Another example of this: at many companies legacy compensation systems have outlived their utility. Many companies still take a conservative approach, whereby most employees come to expect something like a 2 percent or 3 percent raise every year. Says Irv Becker, a compensation expert at the Hay Group, "Taking the middle ground for pay may be the safe ground, but that's not necessarily going to lead to success for your organization. You won't be able to attract the best talent if you're plain vanilla." Compare this with the aggressive way tech companies reward their talent. These companies give their employees an average of 5 percent of revenue in stock-based compensation. That's five times the average of non-tech companies, according to Bloomberg.

A talent-driven company needs a clear but flexible approach to compensation and careers, something that incentivizes everyone to perform well and upgrade their skills, and that keeps top performers from defecting by rewarding them based on their contribution and their market value. Once again, this isn't a once-size-fits-all matter. The comp systems at a trucking company, a fashion retailer, and a computer manufacturer are likely to be quite different, for good reasons.

Still, certain common themes emerge as companies adjust their compensation systems for this talent-driven era. Some companies, especially in the technology world, are doing away with performance-related bonuses. Instead, they offer a competitive base salary and peg bonuses, which are sometimes paid in restricted shares or options, to the company's overall performance. Buttressed by a review system that gives them steady feedback, employees are free to focus on doing great work, to develop, and even to make mistakes without worrying that a subjective rating might knock a percentage point off their pay in the coming year.

Google's former CHRO Laszlo Bock believes in "paying unfairly." In his book, *Work Rules!*, he writes that: "At Google, we . . . have situations where two people doing the same work can have a hundred times difference in their impact, and in their rewards. For example, there have been situations where one person received a stock award of $10,000, and another working in the same area received $1,000,000."[1] This isn't the norm, but bonuses for the best performers are often five times higher than for the rank and file. High-performance workers at junior levels in the company can make more than average performers working at higher levels. Bock strongly believes that it is fairer to pay the best workers significantly more than to pay everyone roughly the same.

There's a certain logic to Bock's approach. A 2012 report from Longwood University's Ernest O'Boyle and Indiana University's Herman Aguinis analyzed human performance across various fields, from academia to professional sports. The authors found that: "Ten percent of productivity comes from the top percentile, and 26% of output derives from the top 5% of workers."[2] This means that "the top 1% of workers generate 10 times the average output, and the top 5% more than four times the average."

Writes Bock, "How many people would you trade for your very best performer? If the number is more than five, you're probably underpaying your best person. And if it's more than ten, you're almost certainly underpaying. It's hard to have pay ranges where someone can make two or even ten times more than someone else. But it's much harder to watch your highest-potential and best people walk out the door."

This is the cold, hard logic of the modern talent marketplace. Don't stick with a middling compensation system and then bemoan the departure of your key employees. The Google attitude is spilling over to more and more companies, which are coming up with their own new ways to reward top talent. GE has created the Chairman's Award, which grants top performers options packages that vest over five years. At Marsh, ex-CEO Peter Zaffino and CHRO Mary Anne Elliott put together a $2.5 million bonus pool for 206 top performers, on top of the company's regular bonus pool. "Companies don't do enough to differentiate their top performers," says Zaffino. "Sometimes those high-potentials don't see a path forward, but if suddenly they're being recognized and rewarded outside of the regular organization, it leads to incredible engagement."

Giving talent a path forward often means giving employees an alternative to conventional career advancement. In traditional companies, talented employees are often promoted into management roles, which are highly compensated. But in Silicon Valley, a top programmer can make far more money than top managers. In worlds where superior talent is everything, such as fashion, entertainment, and sports, paying more for talent is the norm: the coach of the Cleveland Cavaliers does not make more money than LeBron James, nor should he. Don't be locked into traditional thinking about career paths. If you want to scale the individual talent in your company, embrace the idea that you'll need to reward that talent in new and customized ways.

Train Everyone, All the Time

Beth Amato is CHRO of United Technologies Corporation (UTC), a $57 billion manufacturer of aerospace and building equipment. UTC is one of those companies that has replaced a static performance-management system with a dynamic, interactive one. As part of the system, team leaders meet one-on-one with their staffers at least three times a year. What gets discussed in those meetings gets summarized in a single-page document stored in an HR analytics program designed by Workday, an enterprise cloud-software company. Amato wants these get-togethers to be about much more than mere performance evaluation. "People want to improve their careers," she says, "and these meetings make sure they get the training they need. The number-one reason employees leave the company is not pay but whether they have a good relationship with their supervisor and whether they feel they have the ability to advance their career."

Training can't be a sideline enterprise at a talent-driven company. Just as important, training can't be limited to your critical 2 percent. Skills obsolescence is a reality for everyone everywhere, from the factory floor to your office. The pace of technological change is so furious that the process of upgrading the capability of your people needs to be built into the daily fabric of your organization. CFOs must grasp this, so they can set budgets to allow for it. In fact, the G3 should know how much is being spent on training and development, what specifically it's being spent on, and what the company is getting in return for its investment. It helps to build a scorecard to measure how relevant and effective these initiatives are to your company's goals. Once again, think of the analogy to capital deployment. Unlike factories, trucks, and advertising campaigns, people appreciate in value. Investments in training are strategic bets on your most valuable assets.

Targeted precisely, training can enable talent in different ways. Pfizer CFO Frank D'Amelio is one of those finance leaders who speaks the language of his CHRO. "As CFO," he says, "one of my major roles is to maximize the deployment of capital. And I want to be clear—I don't limit that to financial capital. It's all capital, including human." Pfizer spends more on training than when D'Amelio arrived from Alcatel-Lucent a decade ago, and the CFO fully supports the increase. "We have four strategic imperatives," he explains. "One is to foster an 'OWN-IT' culture: 'O' as in 'own the business.' 'W' means 'win in the marketplace.' 'N' means 'no jerks.' 'I' is 'impact the business.' 'T' is 'trusting people.' All training reinforces that 'own-it' culture. We're training with head, heart, and guts." The result: training that helps build a talent-friendly culture, a crucial factor in attracting and retaining the best and the brightest.

At GE, training keeps talent up-to-speed technologically. CHRO Susan Peters knows that trends like the internet of things, cybersecurity, and data mining will touch every job in the company. Part of her job, she explains, is to keep GE competitive by making sure its people learn how to operate in a digital world. "You need a culture across the entire spectrum that understands digital," she says. "That means technical capabilities, but it also requires a shift in mindset. Both require lots of training." GE now blends digital content into the courses offered at its Crotonville leadership institute and around the world. A "Digital Bootcamp" for the company's top seven hundred executives was over-subscribed. GE has even taught coding to its audit staff. "The key is to spread the digital teaching throughout the organization," she says.

AT&T CEO Randall Stephenson spends some $250 million a year training his over 260,000 employees. Back in 2011, he and CHRO Bill Blase realized that the staff lacked two critical things: a knowledge of where the company was headed, and the increasingly specialized skills needed to get there. They've addressed both problems with a systematic training and development program called Workforce 2020.

Workforce 2020 is built around software that's accessible to any employee. Workers can log on to learn what skills the company believes will be critical in the next five years, and what training is available to develop those skills. Blase and Stephenson knew that hands-on help is also invaluable to staffers trying to prepare themselves for the future, so they created "role-based training," which allows staffers to sit down face-to-face with managers around the company to get advice on the skills they need to move into possibly new and different areas. Working closely with HR, employees develop a clear sense of which skills they need to develop.

Once they settle on the kind of training they'd like, employees can sign up for an enormous range of offerings through Workforce 2020. The transformation series, for example, features ninety-minute webinars on new technologies, products, marketing trends, and more. AT&T has partnered with Udacity, an e-learning company, to offer specialized classes in topics such as cybersecurity and the internet of things. AT&T will even pay for employees to get their master's degrees online, from schools such as Georgia Tech and the University of Oklahoma.

"This isn't a one-off exercise," says Blase. His HR department works closely with leaders in the company's technology-operations group to be sure AT&T is always offering training in the most important technologies of tomorrow. "The HR and tech people see this as a continuous process," he says. "It's baked into the way we do business."

At most companies, little effort is put into measuring the effect of the training offered employees. Not so at AT&T. Blase and his HR team created a data-analytics dashboard that focuses on four key measures: awareness, participation, engagement, and competency. The dashboard gives Blase, and Stephenson, a rich portrait of AT&T's evolving workforce. Looking at the results from 2015 and 2016, Blase reports that the company has trained over eighty thousand workers, that engagement is up, and that the company is hiring fewer outsiders, since staffers who have completed the training can fill challenging new roles. There's even a nice little side benefit: "Word is spreading that, 'if I do the training, it will help my career.'"

Getting Started

Talent development is an afterthought at so many companies. But why? If you truly believe that talent is what drives value, it stands to reason that you would do everything you can to maximize the potential of that talent. In this chapter, we've looked at what's required to make talent development the lifeblood of a company that can thrive in chaotic times.

Once again, your first step is to be sure your company is technologically equipped for this task. Predictive analytic software can help you find the right roles for talented employees, spotlight weaknesses they need to address, and forecast the skills they'll need for the future. There are lots of good applications for managing and developing talent. You should ask your CHRO to assemble a portfolio that will inform and improve your talent decisions, and also to give you regular updates on what kind of tangible return you're getting on that investment.

Second, you must rigorously reexamine your company's legacy processes. Career paths, compensation, and talent reviews need to be brought into the twenty-first century. These are the kinds of difficult people decisions that are easy to put off, but the more you delay action, the more you'll feel the friction created by processes designed in more stable times. Your CHRO and your revamped HR department should be your partners in this reexamination. The more they understand the needs of the business, the more aggressive they'll be about replacing worn-out standards with new ones. Remember, people almost always resist changes to practices they've grown accustomed to over the years—but once they experience the benefits of new and streamlined processes, they can quickly adapt.

Third, try to instill a mentality across the company that everyone should be constantly developing his or her skills. Employees tend to be receptive to programs that will expand their potential, but management often fails to spend the time needed to customize training. There are a variety of ways to overcome this pushback, including judging your leaders by the number and quality of leaders they develop.

Together, these steps will give employees the sense that they work for a company that believes in continuous learning and opportunity. These moves quicken the pulse of a company, and help the company have the nimble urgency needed to compete successfully.

But here's the rub: even after all that, you'll inevitably have to reach outside the company for cutting-edge talent. In the next chapter, we'll look at what it takes to have a successful M&A strategy for talent.

Create an M&A
Strategy for Talent

In 2010, Ford Motor, then in the early stages of recovering from the financial crisis that had hammered Detroit's Big Three, sold Volvo to a Chinese auto manufacturer, Geely. Volvo was a mid-market player, with a brand stuck between a rock and a hard place. Its cars didn't match up well with those of top luxury brands like Mercedes, BMW, and Audi, yet the company lacked the capacity to compete with mass-market leaders like Toyota, Ford, and GM. Making matters worse, the company's workforce was dispirited from layoffs during the financial crisis, and ill-prepared for the future. Under Ford, managers had grown accustomed to following the dictates of supervisors in Detroit. Geely wanted its new acquisition to be more independent, a change that was welcomed by top management. But the entrepreneurial sensibilities needed to make the most of having its destiny in its own hands were sorely lacking at Volvo.

At a meeting in the winter of 2011, Volvo's new board of directors (all but one had been appointed after the acquisition) approved a bold strategy and set of goals. Volvo would try to become a premium player. It might sell fewer cars, but at significantly higher margins. Geely backed the plan with an $11 billion commitment to redesign the company's entire product line.

Volvo CHRO Björn Sällström and then-CEO Stefan Jacoby understood the depth of the challenge. Sällström had used a McKinsey tool—the Organizational Health Index—to survey his workforce and measure the organization's capabilities. The results were crystal clear: to move into the premium-brand tier, Volvo needed new people with different skills. "Technically, cars today are very different from ten years ago," says Sällström. "Once, you needed mechanical engineers. Today, there's a greater need for software engineers because cars are computers more than anything else. And now you have electric power trains, autonomous driving, and smart safety features." At a board meeting that spring, Sällström presented his findings. He argued that the new strategy would succeed only with a massive, and swift, infusion of fresh talent. The board agreed, as did the autoworkers' union. Says Sällström: "They saw that if we didn't change, the company wouldn't survive."

In retrospect, getting buy-in was the easy part. Volvo's path forward now entailed pulling off three difficult things at once: reallocating lots of people, further disrupting a culture full of workers who'd expected to stay at Volvo for their full careers; importing loads of outside talent with skills the company had never needed in the past; and meshing these newcomers with the insiders in such a way that the new combination would achieve unprecedented efficiency and creativity in competing with the likes of BMW, Mercedes, Porsche, and Audi.

In this chapter, we'll look at how Volvo successfully managed this challenge, and why three of its key tactics can help ensure that your company always has the best people with the most-critical skills, no matter how technology and the marketplace shift. First, Volvo's executive team expanded its peripheral vision, so that it could reach into other industries for the skills it needed. Second, the company transformed M&A into a talent-acquisition machine. Third, and perhaps most important, its CEOs (Håkan Samuelsson replaced Stefan Jacoby in late 2012) put the CHRO at the center of the company's M&A effort. In a world where industry walls are permeable and technology moves at light speed, you must embrace all three steps if you want to keep up with the competition.

How Volvo Transformed Itself from the Outside In

Sällström, Jacoby, and then Samuelsson took on a new, and ongoing, task: mapping which competencies were most important to Volvo while figuring out where to find employees with those skills. This wasn't a simple task, given the technological challenges faced by the auto industry this decade. The CHRO knew that he could find some of this talent at other automakers, but for the most part he would have to go outside of the industry. The cars of the future—connected, autonomous—will be developed by software programmers and roboticists as much as by "car guys." And since the other legacy car companies needed these people as well, Sällström knew he'd have to be creative as he looked far afield.

He raided Google, but not for programmers—instead, he hired sales people and marketers, who brought in a new customer perspective along with significant knowledge of social media and other increasingly important digital tools. For engineers, he hired from Nokia's R&D team. Why take a chance on cell-phone engineers from a company that was facing major performance challenges? Sällström thought that Nokia's engineers, who were accustomed to thinking about what digital forms might appeal to consumers, would take a fresh approach to designing the radio and navigation systems in the company's cars. R&D managers said, "You're nuts; it will never work," recalls Sällström. But he was right. By applying different thinking to a problem that Volvo's engineers had worked on for years, the Nokia team created what Sällström describes as a uniquely advanced radio and navigation system at a competitive price.

The new hires brought new ideas and practices into the company. Sällström and Samuelsson looked to the fashion industry for expertise that could give Volvo's cars a new look. They hired furniture craftsmen to work on interior wood trim. They even shook up the company's managerial ranks with outsiders. To instill a new sense of entrepreneurialism, they looked for executives who had conceived and executed significant strategic shifts at bigger companies. "When we were a division in Ford," says Sällström, "we were required to execute the Ford Motor business strategy. Someone else told you what to do. Now we had to create the strategy. No one told us what to do, or how to succeed." It was an entrepreneurial story that appealed to outsiders who might otherwise have been nervous about joining the automotive industry. Volvo was a relatively small company undergoing a major transition. There were lots of opportunities for outsiders with critical skills to rise through the ranks. Between 2011 and 2015, the company added three thousand new people in engineering and development.

All too often, companies embark on outside hiring sprees without considering two things: how the outsiders will disrupt the existing culture, and how that culture will accept or reject the newcomers. Jacoby, however, adeptly managed this by clearly communicating the company's new direction to employees, and by soliciting the participation of employees who were excited about the shift. He introduced the new strategy at a big launch event for the company's top three hundred employees. Then he and Sällström implemented a range of initiatives designed to shift the staff into a more entrepreneurial mindset. This started with a host of leadership-development activities for those top three hundred people, each of whom was given a personal coach who addressed shortcomings and helped bolster strengths.

Sällström and Jacoby (and then Samuelsson) put the new critical 2 percent into positions where they could be influential. Not content to rely on that group alone to fight the status quo, they communicated their strategy directly to the workforce, in an ongoing way: Sällström and Samuelsson still hold regular live chats with employees, and lunch often with workers from across the company, soliciting comments and questions.

Jacoby also created a thirty-person "catalyst group," composed mostly of younger employees who showed high potential and a forward-looking attitude. They came from all parts of the company, including engineering, design, quality control, and HR. The catalyst group was charged with showing others in the organization that work could be done differently. "We wanted to show," says Sällström, "that we were serious about the reorganization, that from here on in we weren't bureaucratic and we did want things to happen quickly." Empowered by Jacoby and Sällström, the catalyst group immediately started pushing changes. Its members asked why every design change in a car required a dozen signatures, and managed to cut that number in half. Under Ford, Volvo managers had needed five signatures for travel approval. The catalyst group made sure that managers now took responsibility for controlling their own travel costs. "The small things in a transformation," says Sällström, "can send a signal." After two years of getting the company to think more entrepreneurially, the catalyst group disbanded.

This kind of change takes time, and it's still too early to say that Volvo has turned itself around. Says Sällström: "Even with all this outside DNA, it's a long journey to change the mindset of an organization. It's still a work in progress." The early signs, however, are encouraging. Sällström estimates that he has replaced or reassigned 25 percent of the company's five thousand engineers. Volvo has carved out a spot in the competition to introduce autonomous cars. For example, drivers in Sweden will test one hundred of Volvo's autonomous cars on highways. Financial measures are pointing in the right direction as Volvo's profitability rises. The company is well on its way to meeting its goal of selling 800,000 vehicles in 2020, up from 373,000 in 2010, before the reinvention began. Perhaps most telling, however, is the praise that car-review site Edmunds gave to one of the company's new products. According to Edmunds, the XC90 SUV "puts Volvo right back in the game."

Volvo's actions offer a textbook case in how to go outside the company to retool your workforce for a transformational initiative. In the same way that successful companies use M&A to shape their portfolio of businesses and take advantage of market trends, CEOs need to have a strategy for "talent M&A"—that is, how they will aggressively target pools of external talent to keep ahead of new strategic opportunities. Volvo executed well on so many levels. It expanded its talent horizon, reaching into industries that were far afield of its traditional competitive set to import new skills and thinking. The G3 worked together to implement the transition, taking care to make existing employees allies rather than opponents. The CHRO was fully empowered and trusted by the CEO, and earned that trust with good exterior intelligence and a savvy internal touch. The CFO was in the loop, so budgets allowed for the new hires. Volvo took advantage of the power of internal networks by assembling its catalyst group. And the company's complex change didn't create more bureaucracy—when the catalyst group had done its job, it was dissolved. Reaching outside to transform your company is sometimes necessary, but it's always complicated. Volvo offers a road map of how to pull it off.

The War for Talent Will Get More Competitive

There's nothing unusual about the challenge that Volvo faced. Consumers' tastes change faster than ever now. Competitors are sharper and more efficient than ever. Technological threats arise faster than ever. And talent armed with the skills of the future is more in demand than ever. According to a recent

Korn Ferry analysis of 2,100 companies, 41 percent can't find the talent they need, especially in high-tech fields like IT and engineering.

Companies are no longer just competing against their neighbors for talent—they are competing at a global scale. Platforms like LinkedIn have both expanded the geographic scope of recruiting and made it easier for companies to poach from one another. As Peter Ma, the chairman and CEO of China's Ping An Insurance, puts it: "When I am looking for a new employee, I want to hire the *best in the world* for that given job." Thanks to LinkedIn, as well as Facebook, Glass Ceiling, and other websites, it's easier than ever for your rivals to get a good read on whom you're hiring, who's leaving, and what positions you're looking to fill. In other words, your rivals can use these sources to not only get a read on your long-term strategy, but also to compete with you for the sources of talent needed to execute it.

This competition for talent will only be exacerbated by the aging populations in both the developed and developing countries. According to one McKinsey survey, a staggering 87 percent of companies globally are experiencing a talent shortage. By 2020, the global supply of talent could fall short by as many as forty million college-educated workers. No wonder a 2015 survey from the McKinsey Global Institute and Manpower reported that the number-one concern of CEOs was making sure they hired and retained the human capital their company needed.

Automation will make things even tougher. As AI-enabled robots replace more and more employees in lower-level jobs, people whose skills can multiply value—the kinds of skills that can't be automated—will gain significant leverage. Top lawyers, for example, could spend much more time on high-value client work, since low-value, time-consuming case research is becoming automated. Another example might be a data scientist who regularly delivers telling insights that guide sales and marketing decisions. These types of workers have become more valuable—and harder to recruit and retain.

Succeeding in such a competitive climate is challenging. That's why you must execute a successful strategy of steadily finding, hiring, and integrating the great outside talent your company needs. The three steps we highlighted from the Volvo story are critical. First, you must develop keen peripheral vision, the ability to detect shifts that are not directly related to your business but could affect it. Learning broadly and connecting the dots is a critical skill for modern CEOs. It's especially important now that talent is so mobile and industry borders so porous. The skills your company needs most may not be available in your own industry. So, like Volvo's Sällström, who hired from the mobile-phone, fashion, and furniture industries, you and your CHRO must be familiar with a wider range of pertinent talents than in the past, and ready to pounce when a fit between those talents and your company becomes clear. Second, in an era that's increasingly dominated by the power of small teams, new modes of acquiring talent are becoming important. So-called acquihires—the process by which a big company typically buys a smaller one just for its talent, not its products or revenue—should be among the tools in your arsenal. You should be prepared to buy startups, lure whole teams of people from another company, bring contractors under your roof full-time—whatever it takes to get whatever talent you need. Third, and most important, your CHRO must become a full partner in the M&A process. Leaving the CHRO out of the process, as many companies do, can have a dire financial consequence: about half of all acquisitions fail for people reasons. If your CHRO isn't central to the way you acquire outsiders and integrate them into your company, your mergers may be doomed as well.

Develop Peripheral Vision

Peripheral vision is a deeply underrated skill that has never been more important. There are three reasons for this.

First, the next technological breakthrough may come from anywhere. Technology advances when someone transforms an existing technology by adding something extra—a feature or component—that turns it into an altogether new product that does much more for your customer and creates a new, large, and expanding market space. You don't know where that "something extra" is going to come from, so you must tune your antennae into the outside world in order to be ready when it appears. Peripheral vision is behind so much of what Steve Jobs achieved: think of Apple's success moving into industries like music and mobile phones. Unlike many of the early leaders of the personal-computer business, Jobs was deeply interested in the world outside his Silicon Valley environs. His breadth of knowledge helped him understand consumers, and such breadth and understanding were central to his extraordinary ability to create products that appealed to so wide an audience. In this way, he's a model for any CEO.

Second, the delineation between industries is blurring. Ask yourself this question: What's a car company? Uber? GM? Intel? Indonesia's Grab? Avis? China's Didi Chuxing? Each answer is correct. Now, expand the question: What's a transportation company? The names above? SpaceX? Amazon? UPS? Seamless? FedEx? J.B. Hunt? United? Honda? A nameless startup? Correct again. These days, a search engine (Google) can become a mapping giant, and a retailer (Amazon) can become a leading provider of web services. The advance of technology means that your next competitor could be a company you've never heard of—or perhaps your very best customer. To prepare for the unknown competitor, you must expand your field of vision well beyond what you define as your industry.

Third, recruiting is a global endeavor now. Great talent can be found anywhere. So you need to grow accustomed to searching the nooks and crannies your competitors haven't found yet. We know of one software company that has been tracking the progress of an Indian programmer, who is now in college, since he was nine years old. What kind of nose do you and your HR team have for talent in hidden places?

Great peripheral vision requires two things—great data, and a healthy dose of intuition. The data comes from a variety of sources. Competitive-intelligence firms employ skilled journalists who have left that profession to dig into the competition for paying corporations. More and more of this information is available publicly, on company websites and on Facebook, LinkedIn, Glassdoor, and the like. Your CHRO needs to have employees who comb these sites for people, companies, and trends that might affect your company. Like scouts for an army, these employees serve a defensive purpose, warning you of rising threats. For instance, they might notice that a competitor is listing jobs that require the kind of technical skills that your company highly values. But like scouts for a football team, they can serve an offensive purpose, too, by identifying rising talent. As we've discussed earlier, you and your CHRO must turn your HR department into a competitive advantage. This kind of external research must be part of the department's new and powerful arsenal.

It's not enough to simply absorb data from your CHRO. You need to develop your own wide-ranging sources of information, and listen to them. Steve Jobs incessantly pursued conversations with an array of people he respected. Consider this list of some of the people Jobs talked to regularly at different points over his career: President Bill Clinton; Disney CEO Bob Iger; Kōbun Chino Otogawa, a Buddhist guru; semiconductor pioneer Bob Noyce; Bono; adman Lee Clow; venture capitalists like John Doerr; Roger Ames, a music-industry CEO; Andy Grove of Intel; Larry Brilliant, a scientist who helped eradicate smallpox; Bob Weir of the Grateful Dead; Jim Collins, the management author; the Silicon Valley lawyer Larry Sonsini; IDEO's great product designer David Kelley; Regis McKenna, a pioneering marketer; Bill Campbell, a former football coach. How many engineers are on that list? Just two. Jobs had an avid, insatiable need to learn everything he could about the world beyond Apple. It's something to think about: Who do you speak to on a regular basis? Do you really strive to understand the world beyond your company's doors? The future belongs to those who keep learning, and have an incessant drive to search for what is new.

Turning such data into something that gives your company an edge will call on every bit of intuition you have. Think of this as your "connecting-the-dots" mechanism. Finding the links between outside data and your company's internal needs is a necessary and ongoing creative exercise for any modern CEO. Once again, an anecdote about Steve Jobs best illustrates the process.

In the early- and mid-1990s, Jobs and his wife, Laurene, would vacation regularly in France and Italy. Steve—not Laurene—loved visiting the high-fashion stores of Milan and Paris. Quickly pinning down a sales clerk, Jobs would walk through the entire store, asking question after question: Why is the window display so spare? Why are the dresses positioned over here? Why did you put an archway over there? Why are things cluttered here, and yet over there a single pair of shoes is given such generous room? Tell me about the layout, he'd say. Where do you want your customer to go? How do you think she feels as she walks around? What does she see? What do you want her to touch? This would continue until Laurene, who had been patiently minding the children, would finally insist that they leave. They hardly ever bought anything. But Jobs had gotten what he wanted: information.

Years later, when he had stabilized Apple enough to consider building its own retail stores, Jobs drew on all the seemingly esoteric data he had gleaned during these fashion forays. He hadn't done the standard thing: consult the so-called retail experts in his own market. The Circuit Citys and CompUSAs of the time featured cluttered displays of indistinguishable grey boxes, and poorly informed salespeople incentivized to sell as many PCs as possible, regardless of quality. So, when he finally had a chance to open his own stores, Jobs hired Ron Johnson, a Target guy with no meaningful computer experience, and set about creating stores that were utterly unlike anything the technology business had ever seen. Apple stores waste space wantonly; they are as open as a CompUSA was cluttered. Subtle spotlights on his computers make them look like works of art. Employees don't work on commission. Customers are encouraged to hang out. And the sales per square foot of an Apple store blow away not just those of other computer retailers, but of all retailers. The success of the Apple stores is the direct result of peripheral thinking. Jobs went out of his way—literally— to understand the landscape beyond the engineering-centric world of computing.

That same peripheral vision informed his hiring. The iPod, iTunes, and the iPhone would never have succeeded without aggressive hiring from outside the computer world. Jobs brought in teams of programmers with expertise Apple lacked, executives from the music and cellular industries, and engineers from companies he publicly scorned, like Motorola. Apple still hires from disparate industries. Burberry CEO Angela Ahrendts was brought in to run retail, and the company has aggressively recruited from the auto and health-care industries as it considers moves into those fields. It has even hired roboticists from NASA in its efforts to explore the business of self-driving cars. When Jobs led Apple into music, such bold moves into new business segments were shocking. Now that crossing from one industry into another is almost commonplace, peripheral vision is more important than ever.

Acquihires and Other New Ways to Get the Skills Your Company Needs

The auto industry is proof positive that well-defined business segments can be disrupted at any time. In fact, as we noted above, the "auto industry" has become something much more amorphous, where car manufacturers, software programmers, roboticists, and fleet managers compete over what's come to be known as transportation-as-a-service (TAAS).

The competition has been fueled by acquihires. Wanting to develop its own autonomous vehicles, Uber hired forty researchers and scientists from the robotics division of Carnegie Mellon University. In 2017, when Ford decided to inject some Silicon Valley smarts into its own autonomous-vehicle program, it announced that it would acquire a majority stake in a startup called Argo AI, and invest $1 billion in the company over five years. Argo AI was barely a company! It had been founded just a few months before the Ford investment, by Bryan Salesky and Peter Rander, who had led autonomous teams at Google and Uber. Ford's stake in Argo AI is essentially a way of putting Ford's self-driving-car efforts into Salesky and Rander's hands. In early 2016, GM spent over half a billion dollars to acquire its own Silicon Valley startup, Cruise Automation. Also in 2016, Future Mobility, an electric-car startup backed by China's Tencent Holdings, managed to attract several key employees at BMW's "i" division.

Acquihires are common in Silicon Valley, with Facebook and Google leading the way. To cite just one example, in 2014 Google purchased a startup called DeepMind for over $500 million, just to build up its talent focused on machine learning and artificial intelligence. But other industries have also seen prominent acquihires. Large advertising agencies, for example, bring in talent via acquisition often.

Integrating acquihires is a delicate process, one that works only when you are transparent about some critical decisions.

For instance, how fully do you want to integrate the new talent into your organization's mainstream? Some companies choose to leave the new hires in their original setting, believing that this will preserve their entrepreneurial spirit. Others, wanting to give their organization an injection of innovation, try to work the newcomers into the heart of the company. Still others, like General Motors, try a mix of both. When GM bought Cruise Automation, GM CEO Mary Barra knew she wanted some of Cruise's speed, innovation, and entrepreneurialism to rub off on the corporate executives at headquarters in Detroit. So although Cruise has maintained its own San Francisco headquarters, Cruise CEO Kyle Vogt stays in very close touch with two top executives at GM. Also, employees from Detroit often visit San Francisco, and vice versa.

Outside talent must be allowed to make the changes it was brought in for, or the acquisition will fail and the new talent will leave. The G3 must take action if there's too much pushback as the new recruits conceptualize issues and budgets differently, and challenge the constraints they inherit.

At its best, integration of new talent is a process that begins *before* a merger is proposed. Justin Smith, Google's director of corporate-development integration, says there are three key factors for a successful integration. The first and most important rule is that the acquired company must have an engaged sponsor within Google. The sponsor not only advocates for the acquisition but also commits to sticking with the new talent through the integration process. It's a process that can go on for quite some time, with a member of Smith's corporate-development team working alongside the sponsor and the acquired leadership team. Google formally reviews the success of an acquisition after three months, six months, and one year, and sometimes longer for more complex integrations. Second, Google must have clear expectations of its new talent, and it must align on those expectations clearly to ensure that people can be focused and productive. Even in the earliest conversations with potential acquisitions, Google's people are looking for a certain "Googliness," as Smith puts it. Culture fit is a concern from the start. Third comes crisp communications and follow-up, which is critical for startup entrepreneurs who may be wary of the bureaucracy of bigger corporations. This approach applies to all acquisitions, whether of startups with only a handful of employees or of much more established companies like Waze, which Google acquired in 2013.

The clear expectations and ongoing support matter enormously at a place like Google, says Smith: "We're after leaders who have market and technical vision." In other words, Google is bringing in *talent*, and therefore thinks in terms of supporting and encouraging creative individuals with free-ranging minds. "We know that at some point they're probably going to want to do something else," says Smith. "We prefer to keep them here and give them other challenges if we can. So, we're always trying to get ahead of that by supporting them with coaching and helping them to connect with others across the company."

Put Your CHRO at the Center of All M&A Activity

Acquisitions are typically conceived of as financial moves, and the CFO is deeply involved, auditing the target company's financials and projecting the potential value added. If culture and personality issues are considered at all, it's usually much later in the process—often, too late. Many of the problems associated with this would not arise if the CHRO were empowered to be involved at an equally deep level. After all, the CHRO is "the keeper of the culture," as Kurt Kuehn, the former CFO of UPS, told us. "The CHRO is the one who knows the cultural attributes that are needed for the future, who knows what skill sets will be needed to make a merger successful."

In fact, if the CHRO were tasked with going through some of the same processes as the CFO—auditing talent, and projecting the issues of cultural fit that might prevent newcomers from adding value—many ill-conceived mergers might be avoided, and more well-conceived ones would succeed. The CHRO and CFO should oversee every merger *together*, from the planning stages through the onboarding of the incoming talent. You are spending huge sums of money because you expect the talent from a new company to deliver great value. So why in the world would you pursue a merger without positioning your talent leader at the center of everything? As former GE CEO Jack Welch once said, "If you were running . . . the New York Yankees or the Boston Red Sox, would you like to hang out with the head of player personnel or the team accountant? Who would help you bring the best team to the field? Not the team accountant!" When the partners at private equity firm TPG discovered that one of their own, Jim Williams, had a keen eye for talent, they insisted that he sit at the table at the beginning of every deal discussion. They took his advice to heart, walking away from deals when Williams thought the talent was too weak.

There are five reasons to make the CHRO as central to M&A as the CFO.

First, as your eyes onto the outside world, the CHRO can point you toward the talent you need. Peter Fasolo, as we mentioned in chapter 1, is the CHRO of Johnson & Johnson. He's had the job for a dozen years, during which the pharmaceutical industry has been roiled by new competitors, daunting regulations, and acute financial pressure from Wall Street. Not surprisingly, the industry has seen more than its fair share of mergers during that time. J&J itself has acquired eighteen companies since 2005.

All that experience makes Fasolo something of an expert on finding and successfully importing outside talent. For Fasolo, the process starts way before any specific acquisition. It starts with compiling a database of thousands of outside candidates. Fasolo can turn to this database whenever an opening occurs, and search for people who have the necessary talents, skills, and experience.

But a CHRO isn't just a resource for individual hires. At BlackRock, McGraw-Hill, J&J, and other companies, the CHRO also advocates for mergers and acquisitions. By cobbling together a deep, expansive database of outsiders, a CHRO can see trends in hiring and steer you toward startups that have the best talent in developing fields. This is every bit as valuable as your CFO's ability to pinpoint companies that seem to be a good match for financial considerations.

Second, your CHRO should lead a talent audit of any company you are thinking of acquiring. Surely you would never consider completing a merger without a financial audit conducted under the supervision of your CFO. Yet companies rarely conduct talent audits, even though the financials are unsustainable without great and motivated people. Talent and finance should be considered together.

Preparation, on many fronts, is the key to making a merger work. The G3 must draw a blueprint of what the combined company will look like. The CHRO's part in this is to anticipate and address the many potential personnel roadblocks that may arise. Do the informal networks in the two companies complement one another? What is the structure of work teams in the target company? Who from the acquired company belongs in the critical 2 percent of the combined company? Whose skills from the existing 2 percent will be made redundant by the merger? How will compensation be handled if the target acquisition has a radically different approach to compensation?

These questions can't be properly addressed if your CHRO doesn't have a clear picture of the talent being absorbed. That's why a talent audit should be launched as soon as the very top leaders of both companies are comfortable exploring a merger, perhaps with the help of a third party that can bring objectivity and expertise to bear.

Third, your CHRO should lead the battle to retain the new 2 percent. Talent retention is critical to any merger, especially at the beginning. Once the news is out that you are exploring a merger, your talent is vulnerable. Existing employees may worry about their standing in the new company, question the value of their unvested stock, wonder whether their power will decrease, and doubt the intentions of the other party. Those coming in may be wary of a different culture, and they may assume you have an inherent bias favoring your current talent.

Your CHRO should lead the effort to assuage everyone's worries. Given the eccentricity of today's workplaces, that means designing flexible, customized compensation packages and being transparent about the range of opportunities available to top talent. As we mentioned earlier, you must be prepared to pay "unfairly" if you believe that great talent (of whatever level) creates multiples of value more than average talent (of perhaps even higher level within the organization). This is especially true when your company is undergoing a significant structural change. Whether your best talent comes from the outside or inside, your goal should be to provide that talent with a clear and promising picture of its role in the new organization. Armed with a clear map created with the information from the talent audit, your CHRO can paint that picture better than anyone.

This isn't to say that you should not be deeply involved in retention efforts yourself. As a merger progresses, your most talented employees should see that you are doing everything you can to keep them. As TPG's Williams told his colleagues when he spotted an A-team, "Our challenge is going to be to keep them and connect with them and make sure we love them." Make yourself available for discussions with anyone from the critical 2 percent. Have lunch or dinner with groups of employees, giving them a clear sense of how the merger will benefit them. If you don't give the retention effort your all, you aren't doing everything you can to make the merger work.

Fourth, your CHRO should direct the armies that are going to make the merger work. To ensure that Volvo's turnaround worked, CHRO Björn Sällström and then-CEO Stefan Jacoby created a thirty-person catalyst group to drive efficient processes throughout the changing company. As a merger is getting completed, a good CHRO will have teams of employees with specific assignments ready to make the integration work. The goal is to align old and new employees on the structure, processes, networks, and teamwork that will guide the new organization.

Relying on teams to drive the kind of change you want is a complicated process. Your CHRO needs to be very hands-on during this integration period. He'll have to carefully consider the makeup of these groups, for example. The teams should have employees from both companies, of course, but what kind of employees? It's up to your CHRO and his HR team to see that one team isn't overloaded with leaders while another is made up of nothing but wallflowers. (Your CHRO should know which introverts have great ideas, in order to place those introverts with teams that will be receptive to their quiet value.) It's also up to the CHRO to give teams clear assignments customized to the talents of their members. A "team of teams" can drive integration very efficiently if assignments are clear. If, instead, team members are confused about their goals, the "team of teams" can create a fragmentary chaos that sets your merger off on the wrong foot.

Fifth, your CHRO will neutralize the snipers. No company is without its fair share of complainers, that chorus of people who think that you are leading the company astray. These aren't employees with constructive criticism. These are employees who can poison a culture with their constant complaints. They are especially destructive at companies that depend on small teams, where the negative presence is magnified in a way that can drain team members and throw the creative process off track. Their effect is especially magnified when new employees are joining the company. As we've said repeatedly, these integrations can be difficult and time consuming. The chaos gives snipers a bigger audience, since their message that things were better before the change seems confirmed by the confusion felt by employees.

Your CHRO and the HR staff need to identify these snipers and either change their behavior or remove them. It's the flip side of managing the critical 2 percent, where HR is trying to customize opportunities that drive value. With a sniper, HR is trying to limit his opportunities to cause any meaningful fallout.

Getting Started

We've spent much time in this book talking about how to elevate the organization you oversee. But understanding, recruiting, and integrating talent from the world beyond the walls of your company is just as critical. Bringing in outside talent is more important than ever. Once upon a time, it was enough—and it was possible—to know where your industry was headed. But now your next competitor could come from anywhere, thanks to technology.

That's why widening and extending your peripheral vision is the first step in developing a strategy for always seeking out the best talent anywhere. You and your top executives—especially your CHRO—must make time for learning what's new, what's different, what's about to cross the threshold of your industry.

Peripheral vision is a skill you can develop, and it will lead you to talent that you never knew you needed.

Next, the G3 should commit to a strategy of talent-driven M&A. Acquihires are standard at tech companies that want to surf successfully from one technology wave to the next. The G3 must be just as aggressive. You should be going after top talent all the time, whether or not you have an open slot. And you should be looking in new places, not just relying on the experts within your own industry. Sometimes, the best new ideas are imported from sectors that seem to have little in common with your own.

Put your CHRO at the center of your M&A deliberations. This is a radical change in practice. The fact that CHROs are not already key M&A participants is a surprising oversight, given that so many mergers fail because top talent isn't integrated successfully. But at a talent-driven company in this talent-driven era, doing M&A without the CHRO is like digging for treasure with your bare hands and no map. A CHRO with great peripheral vision will be your guide to the world's best value creators. Just as important, he or she will be the hands-on manager overseeing the addition of newcomers to the delicate lattice that is your organization. Integration of talent is a difficult challenge, one that often determines the success or failure of a merger. Great CHROs that can increase your odds of success with their masterly management of integration certainly deserve to be compensated at the same level as your CFO.

Drive the Talent Agenda

What happens now is all on you.

We aren't trying to be dramatic. But the three of us have been witness to hundreds of corporate reorganizations, and if there's one thing we've learned, it's that these efforts are dead on arrival without the wholehearted, ongoing commitment of the CEO. This has been especially true with human resource initiatives. It's been too easy for CEOs to dismiss these efforts as feel-good morale boosters disconnected from the real work of running the business, and therefore not worthy of much of their valuable time.

That point of view must go. These days, it's fatal to the goals of any company seeking to compete in our fragmented, uncertain economy. As we hope we've made clear in these pages, talent is what drives value today, and great talent properly deployed drives outsize value. You're the only one who can rally the entire workforce behind a talent-first reorganization.

But your job entails far more than cheerleading. You're the one who must redesign the CHRO job and the G3 relationship, establish new paths in and out of HR, approve spending on technology to improve decisions on talent, and follow through as you would on any make-or-break initiative.

The radical transformation you're about to lead will alter the work lives of many in your company—your own most of all. This last chapter is about the kinds of changes you should expect in the content of your daily work. Think of it as a personal checklist of what to expect.

Your Mindset

The central premise of a talent-driven company is that talent drives strategy, as opposed to strategy being dictated to talent. The wrong talent inevitably produces the wrong strategy, and fails to deliver. Numbers like sales and earnings are the result of placing the right people in the right jobs where their talents flourish and they can create value that ultimately shows up in the numbers. Thinking about talent—where to find people with the imagination and skills to propel the company; how to position your critical 2 percent and multiply its impact; what kind of talent the company lacks and how you will get it—becomes Job One. Talent must move to the forefront of your thinking, before strategy, before numbers, before anything else.

As you plan for the next two or three years, looking at what numbers you'll deliver, what funding you'll need, and what capital structure makes sense, the CFO will be at your side. We urge you to bring the CHRO into that loop at the start, not as an afterthought. Don't be frustrated by any initial awkwardness within the G3. Once you and the other members start talking together about talent, strategy, and numbers eight quarters out, you'll find that the combined imagination of the group will open up new possibilities.

Bring talent into quarterly business reviews, and review your top employees at least that often. This isn't just a pro forma review of the performance of your direct reports. You need to do this for everyone in your critical 2 percent. Are these people in the right jobs? What kind of training do they need? If they're not delivering the numbers you expected, why? What can you do to help them? Who needs a stretch challenge? As Aon CEO Greg Case says, "We spend our lives obsessing about how to get everyone to improve, to help them achieve their full potential."

This quarterly review of your talent plan will prompt other important questions to consider. Looking two or three years ahead, will your 2 percenters have the critical skills you'll need? If not, do your competitors' 2 percenters have those skills? If your top people are in something of a slump, why? Has a new technology lessened the importance of their existing abilities? Or is it perhaps that the organizational structure is getting in their way?

These are the questions and decisions that must drive your thinking and actions. In this way, being the CEO of a talent-led organization is like being the coach of a professional basketball team. Your job is to help your greatest talents be as creative and successful as they can be. You want to retain them, but you know we live in a world of free agency, so you're constantly reviewing the data that quantifies their performance, and constantly thinking about who could replace them.

You can help your top talents, but no matter how smart you are, you can't guarantee victory—they're the ones who must make that happen.

The basketball-coach analogy holds up in one other respect. You, too, have assistant coaches. The other members of your G3 will engage all these questions with you. That may take some time to get used to. If you're like most CEOs, it will be tempting to focus primarily on your CFO or COO, who deliver tangible measures of success or failure, the ones Wall Street cares about. You must engage your CHRO equally, however. After all, your CHRO oversees the people who will drive those results. Embracing the G3 concept is the best way to ensure that you're connecting numbers with people. It gives you confidence that your talent will in fact deliver results and create the future. And it reinforces the balanced mindset you need to lead a talent-driven company.

Your Time Allocation

The three of us have found that most CEOs spend their time in fairly predictable ways. Some 40 percent of their time is spent externally, meeting customers or dealing with their board of directors, the media, lobbyists, and regulators. The other 60 percent is focused internally, much of it in regularly scheduled meetings, and some of it dealing with the day-to-day issues that arise unpredictably.

You'll have to reconsider that allocation if you're putting people first. It will be harder than ever to stick to a formulaic or regimented schedule. You'll have to carve out more time for talent issues, such as directly coaching your 2 percent and recruiting from the outside. Coordinating the G3 on talent will be critical—which is why the members' offices should be next to yours, as is the case at BlackRock, McGraw-Hill, and many other companies. You and the other members of the G3 will be partners in reviewing talent, setting and resetting succession plans, promoting leadership development, and defining the key performance indicators and incentives that will help drive the collaborative behavior you want. It's up to you to foster the relationship between the CHRO and the CFO. Each must adapt to the ways of the other. Their employees should work in each other's department. They should speak each other's language. If the CHRO and CFO feel a connection that extends beyond their time with you, and even begin to think of themselves as a unit independent of you, they will become your most valuable tool in leading and changing the company.

Talent once followed finance on the agenda of most CEOs. If you believe that talent drives value, talent should command more of your time than anything else.

Your Sense of the Organization

A talent-driven company built around small teams does away with the command-and-control structure of hierarchical organizations. This will change the way you evaluate the health of your corporation. Focus on the social engine. Is it on a tear or sputtering? Is it creating exponential value? Is it driven by high energy, or inertia? Is it producing new solutions at high speed, or merely riding the momentum of past successes? Is it geared for growth? Infused with the right priorities? More innovative than the social engine of your competitors? Does it have the right level of urgency?

It's never enough to review the numbers without questioning what—or who—is driving them. Are bottlenecks arising that slow decision making, and if so, can you eliminate them? If a division or a team is delivering outsize value, why? What can the rest of the company learn? Thinking of the organization as a living, breathing entity that is driven by talent means staying attuned to its constant changes. Like the human body, the talent-driven organization will react to threats and opportunities before you are conscious of them. The people on the ground can be your early-detection system—if you pay attention.

This is one reason HR needs to be restructured. Talent value leaders—strong, embedded, and empowered—are scouts who can alert top management to the changing needs of your talent, giving you a crisper sense of the trends you must heed. Just as you and your team must stay attuned to changes in the outside world, where new competitors may arise from unpredictable quarters, so too must you stay attuned to the changes inside your company.

A talent-driven organization fosters continuous learning and innovation, and allows breakthroughs to come from unusual places. You can't let leaders get in the way of net-works, relationships, teams, and communication lines that are fluid and open to ideas from outside the traditional chain of command. Otherwise, threats won't be noticed until it's too late, and opportunities will be lost in the fog of corporate inertia.

Your Role as Chief Recruiter

You are your company's top recruiter. You can't just describe the kind of talent you think the company needs, and then rely on HR to go and get it. A talent-first organization is always looking for the best talent, period. People compete, not companies. Each person you hire and develop will either energize or enervate your company. True recruiting is a never-ending task, and a lot more demanding than simply looking for the best person to fill an open slot.

To give you a sense of what this might entail, consider this: we think it's a good idea for you to meet at least monthly with outside talent. These meetings may or may not turn into something tangible. But they serve a secondary purpose: fine-tuning your peripheral vision, improving your sense of the competition and the rising trends that might reshape your business. Turning your attention to the outside world this intently isn't merely an exercise in recruiting, and it isn't optional. Staying attuned to external talent is a critical part of leading a talent-driven company. Innovation and value are created by talent. Finding that talent, wherever it is, is one of your core responsibilities. Your CHRO, of course, will take the lead in building your database of external talent. And as we've mentioned, it's important for you to use the board of directors as a key recruiting tool. But there's only one chief recruiter: you. It's a job that is at least as important as any of your other external roles, including your ambassadorial service to the investment community and the media.

Masahiko Uotani, CEO of Shiseido, has been transforming the 150-year-old Japanese cosmetics company ever since he arrived from Coca-Cola three years ago. Uotani has thrown himself into recruiting. He believes people lead strategy, and is intent on filling Shiseido with "people who can generate better ideas than other people." Uotani looks for three things when he interviews candidates: subject expertise, the ability to teach others and develop new leaders, and the willingness to share the company's commitment to a single Japanese word: *kokorozashi*. Uotani says, "It's a complicated word, and difficult to translate, but I like it. Sometimes it is translated as commitment or vision, and it is similar. But it's more like determination, personal determination." He pauses, and then continues: "You know, if they don't have that, even if they are a great strategist or technical person, he or she shouldn't join us. I don't want people who make me compromise." Uotani knows that bringing in the wrong people could undermine Shiseido's collective commitment to *kokorozashi*. That's why he's on the front lines of the company's recruiting.

In your case, the chief-recruiter role also extends *internally*. Losing key talent is a disaster on par with losing top customers. Your interest in career progression and compensation plans can help retain people over the long haul. But you will also be called in repeatedly on individual cases where someone is considering leaving. This happens now, of course. But you should make yourself more available for these kinds of interventions, and let your CHRO know that you will do your best to keep anyone in the critical 2 percent from going elsewhere. Part of this, of course, is continually giving talent—especially young talent—the sense that your company is a place of limitless opportunity. "Most places in life are continually telling you that your dreams aren't possible or practical," Steve Jobs once said.

"You don't want to hear that when you're under thirty. What you want to do is race after it."

Former Diebold Nixdorf CEO Andy Mattes is convinced that the CEO must be the company's chief recruiter. Mattes, who replaced all but two members of the executive team he inherited, is hands-on with hiring for the top three levels of executives, a group that approximately corresponds to the company's critical 2 percent. He agrees with Jobs: "The CEO can better express aspirational targets than anyone else in the company," he says. "In addition, the CEO is the best talent scout a company can have, given the high visibility we have in the market and all the meetings we have with customers, investors, and partners."

Maggie Wilderotter, the former CEO of Frontier Communications, got involved in filling the top fifty or so jobs, and occasionally reached even deeper into the organization. Why? "It was so important to be sure we had the diversity, experience, and capability," she says. "And I always vetted for values."

The importance of your role as recruiter cannot be overstated. In a talent-driven organization, recruiting is never simply a matter of filling slots. Recruiting will define the future of your company, in everything from innovation to culture.

Your Use of Data

Recognize the continuous stream of HR analytic tools coming on the market and the virtues of creating a digital people platform, and work with your CFO to be sure you're making the appropriate investments. Good talent data that's expertly interpreted can be your most important competitive advantage. Think of GE, that talent-creation and -development machine. Data about the company's employees is woven into the everyday fabric of decision making. Employees are active participants in the creation of a system that drives decisions about where they work, what training they need, and how they are evaluated. It's a system that improves with the addition of more data, allowing for precisely calibrated talent decisions.

Too many decisions about people wind up being decided by "gut instinct" or "who you know." While these intangibles have their place, data can surface the hidden attributes of your employees and explain not just their performance but the reasons for it. You will need to spend time with the data, to review it carefully and regularly in your G3 meetings. Making this data part of your ongoing information diet may not come naturally, especially if, like most CEOs, you're confident in your intuition about people. But data about talent is becoming mission-critical. This is why we believe that investing in a data center for your company is of paramount importance. Today's software puts judgment on sounder footing. It is part of the arsenal of any leader who's seriously committed to the idea that talent drives strategy and value.

Your Operational Checklist

Every CEO keeps a list of must-do items, whether on paper or in mind. CEOs of talent-driven companies must add to their own a few items that aren't on the lists of other CEOs:

- Hold weekly meetings with the G3 to steer the company.

- Stay constantly involved with those in your critical 2 percent. You should personally know them. You should personally sponsor many of them. And you should constantly be looking outside the organization to add to their ranks.

- Put talent at the center of the board agenda, right up there with strategy and risk and compliance issues.

- When making any strategic move, start with the talent implications—you must know which leaders will drive value.

- Pay as much attention to developing and executing the talent strategy as you do to product strategy or competitive strategy.

Constantly challenging yourself to deliver on these five actions is a great way to ensure that you are creating a talent-driven organization, and are not falling back into old habits. If you're straying from these core actions, you might be losing your focus on what makes a talent-driven company a different—and more modern, and more effective—organism.

Talent is king. But running a talent-driven organization isn't suited for someone who wants to be king of the castle. It's not about commanding people to do things. It's not about judging who belongs where in the hierarchy. It's not about underlings bringing you problems and awaiting your decree.

Instead, successfully leading a talent-first company requires agility, an ability to foster collaboration, calm decisiveness in the face of uncertainty, transparency, and faith—specifically, faith in the transforming potential of the talents of others. It requires enough ego to be comfortable with making the hardest decisions, and enough humility to defer to the brilliance of other people.

These traits are the foundation of successfully leading a talent-first organization. In fact, these are traits you should encourage in leaders throughout your organization. Your talent value leaders from HR, business division heads, platform leaders, and board members should understand that enabling talent can never be about the ego fulfillment of leaders. We live in the gig economy, the sharing economy, "free-agent nation," or whatever moniker you prefer to characterize this era of stiff competition for highly-leveraged talent that is at complete liberty to go where it likes. Running a talent-driven company means living with the idea that the talent will determine the direction and strategy of the organization. As Haier's Zhang Ruimin has said, the goal is to "lose control step-by-step."

That's a somewhat frightening idea for anyone accustomed to top-down leadership. But note the second half of Zhang's quote: "step-by-step." Creating and guiding a talent-first organization is not something you should dive into without forethought. Rather, it is something that must be managed incrementally. The steps we've outlined in this book—committing to the integration of capital and talent, and to having talent drive strategy; designing an agile, flexible corporate structure; continually scaling up individual talent; applying these talent-first principles to M&A and external hiring; and turning HR into a competitive advantage—are each important. But built one upon the other, they trigger a multiplier effect that can exponentially increase the value that your talent delivers to the organization.

And that, of course, is the great promise of leading a talent-first organization: seeing new ideas lead to even better new ideas; watching the creative thinking that you've enabled amplify itself across divisions and varying levels of seniority and expertise; and reaping the benefits of value that arises from expected, and unexpected, parts of your company. Managing a talent-led company isn't for the faint of heart. It requires your constant attention, and an alert agility that lets you react at a moment's notice. Its demands of leadership are particularly challenging. But, of course, that very challenge makes leading a talent-driven company acutely satisfying. When you get it right, you have the feeling that you're firing on all cylinders, that you're alive to the potential within your company every minute of every day. When you get it *right*.

We hope our road map sets you off on a successful journey. The rewards are great.

Good luck.

Notes

Unless otherwise cited, all quotes come from interviews conducted by the authors.

Introduction

1. Ram Charan, "It's Time to Split HR," *Harvard Business Review*, July–August 2014.
2. Ram Charan, Dominic Barton, and Dennis Carey, "People Before Strategy: A New Role for the CHRO," *Harvard Business Review*, July–August 2015.

Chapter 1

1. Leonardo Baldassarre and Brian Finken, "GE's Real-Time Performance Development," *Harvard Business Review*, August 12, 2015, https://hbr.org/2015/08/ges-real-time-performance-development.

Chapter 2

1. Jonathan Bailey and Tim Koller, "Are You Getting All You Can from Your Board of Directors?" *McKinsey Quarterly*, November 2014.

Chapter 4

1. Josh Bersin, "Global Human Capital Trends 2015," Deloitte, https://www2.deloitte.com/content/dam/Deloitte/de/Documents/human-capital/HCTrends%202015%20Report_TuesFeb24.pdf.
2. Korn Ferry Institute, *Real World Leadership* (Korn Ferry report, 2015).
3. Harvard Business Review Analytic Services, "HR Joins the Analytics Revolution," Harvard Business School Publishing, Boston, 2014.

NOTES

Chapter 5

1. Laszlo Bock, *Work Rules!* (London: John Murray, 2015), 241.
2. Ibid.

Index

acquihires, 139, 144–147, 154

ADP, 33

agility, 58–63, 76–77

Alphabet, 4, 59

Amato, Beth, 124

Amazon, 54, 59

Amgen, 68–72, 83–84

annual reviews, 104, 115–116, 118–119

Aon, 19

Apple, 25, 45–46, 55, 59, 140, 143–144

Argo AI, 145

assets, deployment of, 3–4

AT&T, 126–127

auto industry, 144–145

automation, 89–90, 138–139

Bague, Hugo, 80

Barclays Global Investors (BGI), 106

Barra, Mary, 146

Baweja, Sanjay, 17–18

benchmarking, 75–76

Berisford, John, 21–23

BlackRock, 104–109

Blackstone, 27, 36, 41

Blase, Bill, 126, 127

board of directors, 7, 37–56

CEO and, 37–39

CHRO and, 39–41, 48–50, 55

diversity and, 51–53

investors and, 53–55

priorities for, 44–53

reorganization of, 41–44

role of, 37–38

succession planning and, 38, 45–47

top talent and, 47–51, 56

bonuses, 121–123

Bradway, Bob, 69, 70–71

Breen, Ed, 18, 25

Breitfelder, Matt, 106, 108–109

business strategy, 1–2

Callahan, Jack, 21–23

capital

deployment of, 4

financial, 4

human, 3–5

Cardinal Health, 117–118

career development, software tools for, 30

career path

in HR, 91–95, 101

for top talent, 123

Index

Case, Greg, 19

change agents, 70, 72–73

chief executive officer (CEO), 15–18
  board of directors and, 37–39
  as chief recruiter, 161–163
  as driver of talent agenda, 155–167
  former CHROs as, 99
  G3 and, 84
  mindset of, 156–158
  operational checklist for, 164–167
  sense of organization, 159–160
  succession of, 38, 45–47, 98–99
  time allocation by, 158–159

chief financial officer (CFO)
  CHRO and, 7, 20–24, 80, 83–84
  compensation of, 98
  G3 and, 6, 15–18
  role of, 18, 35

chief human resources officer
    (CHRO)
  board of directors and, 39–41,
    48–50, 55
  CEO succession and, 46–47
  CFO and, 7, 20–24, 80, 83–84
  elevation of, 15, 18–20
  G3 and, 6, 15–18
  pay disparities for, 97–99
  qualities of, 81–84
  role of, 8–10, 35
  talent acquisition and, 139–140,
    147–153, 154

Clustree, 111

collaboration, 8

communication, 70, 147

company mission, 68

compensation committees, 7, 42–43,
    55–56

compensation disparities, 97–99

compensation systems, 121–123, 151

competitive advantage
  HR as source of, 79–101
  of talent, 1–2, 12

competitive intelligence, 141–142

complainers, 152–153

Cook, Tim, 46

corporate culture, 69, 71, 147, 148

Costello, Larry, 81–82

critical 2 percent, 6–7, 9, 15
  board of directors and, 47–51, 56
  health of, 47–51
  identifying and cultivating, 24–28
  retention of, 149–150
  value creation by, 24–26, 35–36
  See also talent

crowdsourcing, performance feed-
    back, 116–117

culture transformation, software
    tools for, 31–32

D'Amelio, Frank, 125

data analysis, 31–32, 84–90, 104,
    110–115, 163–164

databases, cleaning up old, 32–33

data sharing, 32–34

Davies, Christa, 19

digital people platform, 32–33

digital technology, 28–36, 88–89,
    125–126

diversity, 51–53

Elliott, Mary Anne, 13–15, 123

embedded analytics, 113–114

employee engagement, 68, 71–72

Employee Management System
    (EMS), 119

employees
  compensation of, 121–123
  negative, 152–153

Index

performance feedback for, 115–123
training, 124–127
executive compensation, 97–99
executive leadership, 6, 13–24

Facebook, 58–63
Fasolo, Peter, 28, 149
Fast Retailing, 72–74
financial capital, 4
Fink, Larry, 105
Ford Motor, 131–132, 145
Future Mobility, 145

G3, 13–24, 35, 80, 84
Geely, 131–132
General Electric (GE), 42–44, 54,
    116, 118–120, 123, 125–126, 164
General Motors (GM), 145, 146
Gerstner, Lou, 25
GlaxoSmithKline, 47, 84
global recruitment, 141
Gogel, Don, 51
Goland, Tony, 19
Goler, Lori, 60, 62–63
Google, 4, 32, 54, 122–123, 134,
    145–147
Goyal, Aadesh, 17–18

Hackamonth program, 61
Haier, 64–67, 78
Hastings, Reed, 116
Haug, Erik, 52–53
hierarchy, 8, 63, 65
horizontal structure, 8
Humana, 92–95
human capital, 3–5. *See also* talent
human capital committee (HCC),
    106–107
human resources (HR)

business talent in, 81–84
career path, 91–95, 101
as competitive advantage, 79–101
data analysis by, 84–90
data for, 32–34
digitization of, 28–35, 36
elevation of, 11–12, 19–20
reinvention of, 8–9, 160
role of, 79–80, 87–88
software tools, 28–35, 100, 110–115
staff, 86–87
strategic side of, 86–88
talent value leaders, 95–97,
    100–101
transactional tasks in, 88–90
Humanyze, 31–32
Huval, Tim, 92–95

influencers, 73–74
ING Group, 49–52
investors, 53–55
Ive, Jonathan, 25

Jacoby, Stefan, 132, 135–136, 151–152
Jauhar, Shakti, 33–34, 86, 90
Jobs, Steve, 25, 45–46, 140, 142–144,
    162–163
Johnson & Johnson, 9, 28, 90, 149

Knaapen, Hein, 49–52
Kuehn, Kurt, 148
Kumar, Vinod, 17–18

Laschinger, Mary, 18
legacy processes, 115–123, 128
Leimkuhler, Courtney, 13–15
LinkedIn, 138
luck, 3
Lund, Susan, 63

Index

Ma, Peter, 138
Macdonald, Randy, 39–40
management development and
    compensation committee
    (MDCC), 42–44
managers, 61–63
market fragmentation, 66
Marsh, 13–15, 123
Mattes, Andy, 163
McGraw, Terry, 21–22
McGraw-Hill, 21–24
McKinsey, 67, 75–76, 89, 112–113
McNamee, Brian, 69–71, 83–84
meaningful work, 67–74, 77
merger and acquisitions (M&As),
    131–154
Microsoft, 116
millennials, 68
mobile apps, 30–31, 88–89
Mulally, Alan, 20

negative employees, 152–153
Netflix, 116
networking strategy, 66
Nissan, Steven, 25
Nokia, 134

Oblong, 112–113
offshoring, 89
Ogg, Sandy, 27, 47
operational checklist, 164–167
Organizational Health Index (OHI),
    75–76
organizational structure, 57–78
    agile, 58–63, 76–77
    flattening of, 8
    meaningful work and, 67–74, 77
    platforms, 63–67, 77
    social architecture, 74–76, 77
outsourcing, 89

Page, Larry, 54
payroll data, 33
PD@GE, 119–120
people committee, 42–43
people-first companies, 5–11, 15. *See
    also* talent-driven organizations
people initiatives, 2
PepsiCo, 33–34, 86, 90
performance development, 120
performance feedback, 115–123
performance management, 30–31,
    115–123
performance-related bonuses,
    121–122
peripheral vision, 10, 139, 140–144,
    153–154, 161
personnel analytics, 114–115
Peters, Susan, 42–43, 119, 120,
    125–126
Pfizer, 125
Phelan, Dan, 47, 84
Pixar, 25
platforms, 63–67, 77
power centers, 27–28
predictive analytics software,
    112–113, 128
product customization, 66

quarterly business reviews, 157

Reardon, Nancy, 48
recruitment, software tools
    for, 29
retention, software tools for, 30
robotic process automation (RPA),
    89–90
role-based training, 126

Sällström, Björn, 132, 133–136, 151–152
Samuelsson, Håkan, 133, 134

Index

Shiseido, 161–162

Siegel, Laurie, 40, 41

Siegmund, Jan, 33

skill obsolescence, 9, 124–125

smartphones, 88–89

Smith, Jeff, 105, 108–109

Smith, Justin, 146–147

social architecture, 74–77, 159–160

social networks, 26–27

software applications, 7, 9, 28–35, 36, 100, 104, 110–115, 164

solution-first approach, 67–68

staff development, 25

startups, 139

Stephenson, Randall, 126

succession planning, 38, 45–47, 98–99, 114

talent

    audit, 148–149

    board of directors and, 38–39, 47–51, 56

    competition for, 137–140

    as competitive advantage, 1–2, 12

    data on, 84–90

    deployment of, 4–5, 108–109

    external, 28, 139, 144–147, 154, 161

    in HR, 81–84

    identifying and cultivating, 24–28

    management of, 2–5, 38–39

    recruitment, 69, 141, 161–163

    retention, 149–150, 162–163

    rewarding, 122–123

    shortages, 138

    trust in, 107–108

    unleashing individual, 103–129

    See also critical 2 percent

talent, strategy, risk (TSR), 7, 38

talent acquisition, 10, 131–154

    acquihires, 139, 144–147, 154

CHRO and, 139–140, 147–153

talent agenda, 155–167

talent and rewards committee, 7, 42–43, 55–56

talent development, 9, 103–129

    at BlackRock, 105–109

    software and data tools for, 110–115, 128

    training, 124–127, 128

talent-driven organizations

    aligning board of directors with, 37–56

    compensation approaches, 121–123

    employees as central to, 68–74

    individual talent in, 103–129

    mindset of, 156–158

    organizational structure, 57–78

    role of CEO in transformation to, 155–167

    role of HR in, 79–101

talent roster, 6–7

talent technology, 7

talent value leaders (TVLs), 95–97, 100–101

Tata Communications (Tatacom), 17–18

team leaders, 61–63

technological change, 124–125, 140

technology

    automation, 89–90

    digital, 28–36, 88–89, 125–126

    human resources, 28–35, 36, 88–89

    talent, 7

Telenor, 41, 52–53

time allocation, 158–159

total shareholder return (TSR), 7, 38

training, 124–128

transparency, 70, 83, 107

Index

transportation-as-a-service (TAAS), 145

Trudell, Cynthia, 33

trust, 107–108

Uber, 145

United Technologies Corporation (UTC), 124

Uotani, Masahiko, 161–162

UPS, 25–26

value creation, 5–6, 12, 24–26, 35–36

VoloMetrix, 30, 112, 151–152

Volvo, 131–137

Waersted, Gunn, 52

Watkins, Carole, 117–118

Welch, Jack, 148

Wilderotter, Maggie, 163

Williams, Jim, 148

Wilson, Ken, 106

women, 51–52, 53

Workforce 2020, 126

workforce diversity, 51–53

Yanai, Tadashi, 72–74

Zaffino, Peter, 13–14, 123

Zalando, 116–117

Zhang, Ruimin, 64–67, 78, 166

Zuckerberg, Mark, 59–60

Acknowledgments

First and foremost, thanks to the many CEOs, CFOs, and HR leaders we spoke with who generously shared their own learning and hard-won experience. Their examples enliven the narrative, enhance the learning for readers, and inspire us all. Our playbook is infinitely richer for their contributions.

Appropriately, a lot of talented people across three very agile organizations shared their time, intelligence, and contacts to help us transform our ideas and experience into a book.

Special thanks to the "core team" who were in there brainstorming approaches or managing the complex logistics of reporting and publishing throughout the journey: Geri Willigan, Cynthia Burr, and Jodi Engleson from Charan Associates; Donna Gregor from Korn Ferry; and Rik Kirkland and Matthew Smith from McKinsey & Company.

In addition, we benefited from a brilliant cast of friends and colleagues who shared their energy and insights—as well as their belief in the importance of this topic—over many months. Dennis's thought partners at Korn Ferry include: Gary Burnison, Stu Crandell, Dave Eaton, Ilene Gochman, Joe Griesedieck, Bob Hallagan, RJ Heckman, Jean-Marc Laouchez, Colleen O'Neill, and Tharuma Rajah.

Acknowledgments

At McKinsey, we drew on the deep, in-the-arena knowledge of leaders and experts from across our organization practice and its talent and human capital service lines. Among them: Chris Gagnon, Neel Gandhi, Judith Hazlewood, Elizabeth Hioe, Conor Kehoe, Scott Keller, Luke Lu, Frithjof Lund, Susan Lund, Dana Maor, Mary Meaney, Bill Schaninger, and Nina Spielmann. Three colleagues played an important role in tracking down data and examples and keeping the trains running down multiple tracks: Claire Colberg, Drew Marconi, and Roni Luo.

Brian Dumaine helped report and capture the first draft of history. Rick Tetzeli's elegant writing and editing contributed enormously to the final shape of the book. Melinda Merino was a key thought partner and passionate believer in this project from day one. She and her dedicated colleagues at Harvard Business Publishing could not have been better partners.

Finally, a special thanks to current and aspiring leaders everywhere who are reading this book in the sincere effort to improve their own contribution to business and society as a whole.

—Ram Charan,
Dominic Barton,
Dennis Carey

About the Authors

Ram Charan is a world-renowned business adviser, author, teacher, and speaker who has spent the past forty years working with CEOs, boards, and executives of the world's top companies. Formerly on the faculties of Harvard Business School and Northwestern University, he is the author of twenty-five books that have sold over four million copies and have been published in over a dozen languages, including the bestselling *Execution*, *Confronting Reality*, and *The Attacker's Advantage*. In addition to advising and coaching leaders, Charan serves on several boards in the United States, Turkey, China, India, and Brazil. He has received best teacher awards from Wharton, Northwestern, and GE's learning center at Crotonville, New York; and in 2005 was elected a Distinguished Fellow of the National Academy of Human Resources.

Dominic Barton is the global managing partner of McKinsey & Company. Since joining the firm in 1986, he has advised clients in a range of industries, including banking, consumer goods, high tech, and industrial. Before becoming global managing director, he was McKinsey's chairman in Asia, based out of Seoul, Shanghai, and Singapore for twelve years. Barton leads McKinsey's work on the future of capitalism, long-term value creation, and the role of business leadership in society. He has authored more than eighty articles on capitalism, leadership, financial market development, Asia, history, and the issues and opportunities facing global and Asian markets, and is the coauthor of three books, including *Reimagining Capitalism.*

Dennis Carey is Vice Chairman of Korn Ferry, where he recruits board directors, CEOs, and their direct reports. He has placed and assessed some of the most successful CEOs and directors for over sixty leading companies in the *Fortune* 500. Carey founded several forums for chairmen, CEOs, and C-suite executives, including The Prium and the CEO Academy, as well as academies for CFOs and CHROs of America's best-managed enterprises. He has published five books and over fifty refereed journal articles covering topics ranging from CEO succession and corporate strategy to M&A, corporate governance, and human capital. His most recent book, *Boards That Lead*, coauthored with Ram Charan and Mike Useem, was cited as book of the year by *Directors & Boards* magazine. Carey also teaches corporate governance at the Wharton School of the University of Pennsylvania, and has held post-doctoral fellowships at Harvard's John F. Kennedy School of Government and Princeton Theological Seminary. He has served on both public and private technology boards.